Papahānaumokuākea Marine National Monument

CONDITION REPORT 2009

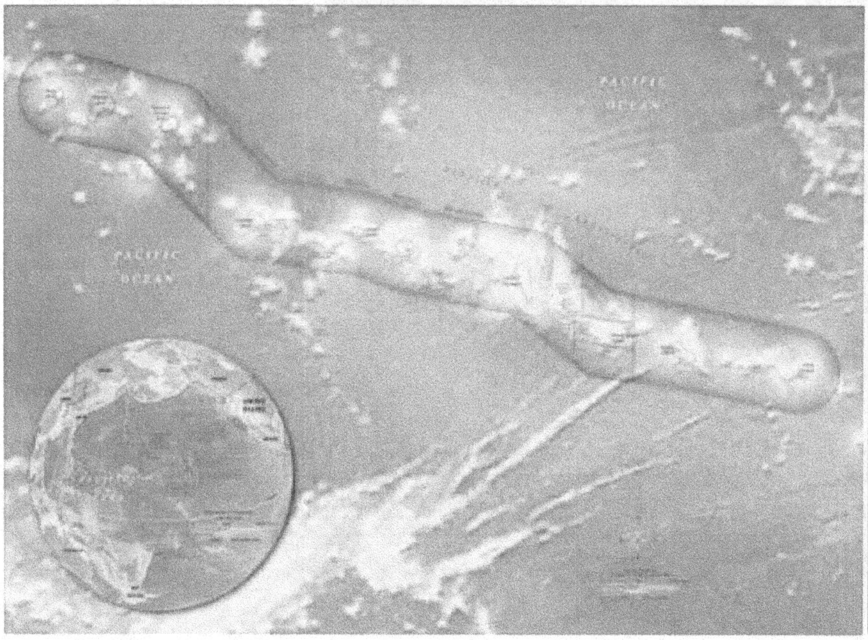

March 2009

NATIONAL MARINE SANCTUARIES

U.S. Department of Commerce
Gary Locke, Secretary

National Oceanic and Atmospheric Administration
Jane Lubchenco, Ph.D.
Under Secretary of Commerce for Oceans and Atmosphere

National Ocean Service
John H. Dunnigan, Assistant Administrator

Office of National Marine Sanctuaries
Daniel J. Basta, Director

U.S. Department of the Interior
Ken Salazar, Secretary

U.S. Fish and Wildlife Service
Rowan W. Gould, Acting Director

Report Preparers:

Papahānaumokuākea Marine National Monument:
Dr. Randy Kosaki, Malia Chow, Elizabeth Keenan

Office of National Marine Sanctuaries:
Kathy Broughton, Dr. Stephen R. Gittings

Copy Editor: Matt Dozier

Graphic Designer: Matt McIntosh

National Oceanic and Atmospheric Administration
Office of National Marine Sanctuaries
SSMC4, N/ORM62
1305 East-West Highway
Silver Spring, MD 20910
301-713-3125
http://sanctuaries.noaa.gov

Papahānaumokuākea Marine National Monument
6600 Kalaniana'ole Hwy, #300
Honolulu, HI 96825
808-397-2660
http://hawaiireef.noaa.gov

U.S. Fish and Wildlife Service
1849 C Street, NW
Washington, DC 20240
800-344-9453
http://www.fws.gov

State of Hawaii
Department of Land and Natural Resources
1151 Punchbowl Street, Rm. 330
Honolulu, HI 96813
808-587-0099
http://www.hawaii.gov/dlnr

NATIONAL MARINE
SANCTUARIES

Cover credits (Clockwise):

Map:
The bathymetric data shown on this map is from the 2-Minute gridded global relief data set, also known as ETOPO2 ver 2. Data and metadata may be obtained from: http://www.ngdc.noaa.gov/mgg/fliers/06mgg01.html

Photos:
Coral reef: James Watt; Hawaiian monk seal: James Watt; Brown booby at Pearl and Hermes Atoll: Dan Suthers; Spinner dolphins: James Watt; Galapagos sharks: James Watt; Dan Suthers; Bow of the USS *Macaw*: James Watt

Suggested Citation:
Office of National Marine Sanctuaries. 2009. Papahānaumokuākea Marine National Monument Condition Report 2009. U.S. Department of Commerce, National Oceanic and Atmospheric Administration, Office of National Marine Sanctuaries, Silver Spring, MD. 54 pp.

Table of Contents

About this Report

This "condition report" provides a summary of the status of the resources in the Papahānaumokuākea Marine National Monument, which is co-managed by National Oceanic and Atmospheric Administration, the U.S. Fish and Wildlife Service and the State of Hawaii. The report includes pressures on the monument resources, current condition and trends, and management responses to the pressures that threaten the integrity of the marine environment. Specifically, the document includes information on the status and trends of water quality, habitat, living resources and maritime archaeological resources and the human activities that affect them. It presents responses to a set of questions posed to all sanctuaries (Appendix A). Resource status of Papahānaumokuākea Marine National Monument is rated on a scale from good to poor, and the timelines used for comparison vary from topic to topic. Trends in the status of resources are also reported and are generally based on observed changes in status over the past five years, unless otherwise specified. Monument staff consulted with a working group of outside experts familiar with the resources and with knowledge of previous and current scientific investigations. Evaluations of status and trends are based on interpretation of quantitative and, when necessary, non-quantitative assessments and the observations of scientists, managers and users. The ratings reflect the collective interpretation of the status of local issues of concern among monument program staff and outside experts based on their knowledge and perceptions of local problems. The final ratings were determined by sanctuary staff. This report has been peer-reviewed and complies with the White House Office of Management and Budget's peer review standards as outlined in the Final Information Quality Bulletin for Peer Review.

This is the first attempt to describe comprehensively the status, pressures and trends of resources at Papahānaumokuākea Marine National Monument. Additionally, the report helps identify gaps in current monitoring efforts, as well as causal factors that may require monitoring and potential remediation in the years to come. The data discussed will enable us not only to acknowledge prior changes in resource status, but will also provide guidance for future management challenges.

Summary and Findings

Papahānaumokuākea Marine National Monument (the monument) is the single largest conservation area under the U.S. flag, encompassing 139,792 square miles of the Pacific Ocean - an area larger than all the country's national parks combined. Thanks to their isolation and past management efforts, the reefs of the Northwestern Hawaiian Islands are considered to be in nearly pristine condition. Home to the highly endangered Hawaiian monk seal, threatened green sea turtles and high abundances of endemic species (found nowhere else on earth), the complex and highly productive marine ecosystems of the Northwestern Hawaiian Islands are significant contributors to the biological diversity of the oceans (Friedlander et al. 2005.)

Due to the monument's remoteness and regulations that limit access, impacts from local human uses are relatively few. However, past activities have permanently altered some areas and in some cases resulted in degradation of habitats. Also, human activities currently taking place outside the monument, such as deposition of marine debris, can result in living resource, habitat, and water quality degradation. Other concerns for the monument include climate change and coral bleaching, diseases affecting marine organisms, and marine alien species that can threaten native biodiversity and degrade habitats.

Despite past human uses such as military activities that have left behind contamination on many of the atolls, monument-wide water quality parameters suggest relatively good conditions, due primarily to the monument's remoteness and current regulations that limit access. Habitat structure has been impacted by derelict fishing gear, marine debris and coral bleaching. However, a majority of these habitats have not been significantly affected and are in good condition. Most living resource populations in the monument appear to be in healthy condition; however, monk seals are significantly decreasing. Other significant threats include potential manifestations of global climate change such as seawater acidification, rising sea surface temperatures and rising sea levels. The monument's management plan, released in December 2008, recommends a number of management actions that will address these concerns.

Papahanaumokuakea
Marine National Monument

- *139,797 square miles of land and ocean and is the single largest conservation area under the U.S. flag*

- *Designated by Presidential Executive Order in 2000 as a Coral Reef Ecosystem Reserve; subsequently designated by Presidential Proclamation as a Marine National Monument in 2006*

- *Among the few large-scale, intact, predator-dominated reef ecosystems left in the world*

- *High incidence of marine endemism due to the age of the islands and relative isolation from other coral reefs*

- *A rich cultural history of deep ties between Native Hawaiians and the land and ocean, on genealogical, cultural and spiritual levels that remain today*

Spinner dolphins use the shallow lagoons of the atolls to rest during the day, and feed in the deeper waters surrounding the atolls at night.

Information regarding maritime archaeological resources is limited due to the size of the monument. However, known resources do not appear to be a threat to the environment, and there is very little human activity that may threaten the integrity of archaeological resources. The primary threat to these resources is their natural deterioration over time; little can be done to control or protect these resources from natural processes.

National Marine Sanctuary System and System-Wide Monitoring

The National Marine Sanctuary System manages marine areas in both nearshore and open ocean waters that range in size from less than one to almost 140,000 square miles. Each area has its own concerns and requirements for environmental monitoring, but ecosystem structure and function in all these areas have similarities and are influenced by common factors that interact in comparable ways. Furthermore, the human influences that affect the structure and function of these sites are similar in a number of ways. For these reasons, in 2001, the program began to implement System-Wide Monitoring (SWiM). The monitoring framework (NMSP 2004a) facilitates the development of effective, ecosystem-based monitoring programs that address management information needs using a design process that can be applied in a consistent way at multiple spatial scales and to multiple resource types. It identifies four primary components common among marine ecosystems: water, habitats, living resources and maritime archaeological resources.

By assuming that a common marine ecosystem framework can be applied to all places, the National Marine Sanctuary System developed a series of questions that are posed to every sanctuary and used as evaluation criteria to assess resource condition and trends. The questions, which are shown on the following pages and explained in Appendix A, are derived from both a generalized ecosystem framework and from the National Marine Sanctuary System's mission. They are widely applicable across the areas managed by the National Marine Sanctuary System and provide a tool with which the system can measure its progress toward maintaining and improving natural and archaeological resource quality.

Similar reports summarizing resource status and trends will be prepared for each marine sanctuary approximately every five years and updated as new information allows. The information in this report is intended to help set the stage for the management plan review process. The report also helps sanctuary staff identify monitoring, characterization and research priorities to address gaps, day-to-day information needs and new threats.

Papahānaumokuākea Marine National Monument
Condition Summary Table

The following table summarizes the "State of Monument Resources" section of this report. The first two columns list 17 questions used to rate the condition and trends for qualities of water, habitat, living resources, and maritime archaeological resources. The Rating column consists of a color, indicating resource condition, and a symbol, indicating trend (see key for definitions). The Basis for Judgment column provides a short statement or list of criteria used to justify the rating. The Description of Findings column presents the statement that best characterizes resource status, and corresponds to the assigned color rating. The Description of Findings statements are customized for all possible ratings for each question. Please see Appendix A for further clarification of the questions and the Description of Findings statements.

Status: | Good | Good/Fair | Fair | Fair/Poor | Poor | Undet. |

Trends:
Conditions appear to be improving .... ▲
Conditions do not appear to be changing .... −
Conditions appear to be declining .... ▼
Undetermined trend .... ?
Question not applicable .... N/A

#	Questions/Resources	Rating	Basis for Judgment	Description of Findings	Monument Response
WATER					
1	Are specific or multiple stressors, including changing oceanographic and atmospheric conditions, affecting water quality and how are they changing?	▼	Published literature indicates temperature increases.	Selected conditions may preclude full development of living resource assemblages and habitats, but are not likely to cause substantial or persistent declines.	Monitoring of physical and biological parameters to evaluate extent of the issue.
2	What is the eutrophic condition of monument waters and how is it changing?	−	Lack of anthropogenic inputs.	Conditions do not appear to have the potential to negatively affect living resources or habitat quality.	Monument designation regulates access and requires reporting for on-going monitoring.
3	Do monument waters pose risks to human health and how are they changing?	−	Lack of sources, causes and human exposure.	Conditions do not appear to have the potential to negatively affect human health.	No current issues.
4	What are the levels of human activities that may influence water quality and how are they changing?	▲	Limited access; regulations prohibit discharges.	Few or no activities occur that are likely to negatively affect water quality.	Continuous evaluation of possible impacts of ship traffic.
HABITAT					
5	What are the abundance and distribution of major habitat types and how are they changing?	▼	Marine debris is degrading beaches and reefs. Potential loss of habitat from climate change and sea-level rise.	Selected habitat loss or alteration has taken place, precluding full development of living resource assemblages, but it is unlikely to cause substantial or persistent degradation in living resources or water quality.	Active detection and removal program to reduce accumulations of marine debris. Monitoring of physical and biological parameters of climate change.
6	What is the condition of biologically-structured habitats and how is it changing?	▼	Marine debris, coral disease and perhaps bleaching frequency.	Selected habitat loss or alteration has taken place, precluding full development of living resources, but it is unlikely to cause substantial or persistent degradation in living resources or water quality.	Supporting research to better understand the impacts. Development of best management practices to minimize transfer between sites.
7	What are the contaminant concentrations in monument habitats and how are they changing?	−	Localized contamination is adversely affecting associated habitat and wildlife.	Selected contaminants may preclude full development of living resource assemblages, but are not likely to cause substantial or persistent degradation.	No management response.
8	What are the levels of human activities that may influence habitat quality and how are they changing?	−	Limited visitation.	Some potentially harmful activities exist, but they do not appear to have had a negative effect on habitat quality.	Rigorous permitting and monitoring of human activities to ensure limited cumulative effects.

Table is continued on the following page.

Papahānaumokuākea Marine Monument Condition Summary Table (Continued)

#	Questions/Resources	Rating	Basis for Judgment	Description of Findings	Monument Response
LIVING RESOURCES					
9	What is the status of biodiversity and how is it changing?	–	Assessment/monitoring activities to date.	Biodiversity appears to reflect pristine or near-pristine conditions and promotes ecosystem integrity (full community development and function).	Continuing efforts to characterize biodiversity.
10	What is the status of environmentally sustainable fishing and how is it changing?	▲	Limited activity; existing fishery to be phased out by June 2011.	Extraction does not appear to affect ecosystem integrity (full community development and function).	Developing fisheries independent stock assessment methods that will be implemented post fishing cessation.
11	What is the status of non-indigenous species and how is it changing?	?	Few species with isolated distributions; uncertainty of potential impact.	Non-indigenous species exist, precluding full community development and function, but are unlikely to cause substantial or persistent degradation of ecosystem integrity.	Prevention through hull inspections and cleaning, marine debris removal, quarantines in place for most islands; monitoring programs may document distribution and abundance of non-indigenous species.
12	What is the status of key species and how is it changing?	?	Monk seal decline; corals and predatory fish populations high and stable.	The reduced abundance of selected keystone species may inhibit full community development and function and may cause measurable but not severe degradation of ecosystem integrity; or selected key species are at reduced levels, but recovery is possible.	Mitigation efforts include predator removal and seal relocation to improve survivorship. Implementation of recovery plans for monk seals and ongoing research to understand foraging, diet and habitat.
13	What is the condition or health of key species and how is it changing?	?	Monk seal starvation and body condition; debris ingestion by seabirds; predatory fish and most corals in good condition and stable.	The diminished condition of selected key resources may cause a measurable but not severe reduction in ecological function, but recovery is possible.	Intense research and monitoring target of key endangered species.
14	What are the levels of human activities that may influence living resource quality and how are they changing?	–	Limited visitation.	Some potentially harmful activities exist, but they do not appear to have had a negative effect on living resource quality.	Through regulated activities visitation is monitored to ensure that impacts are minimized.
MARITIME ARCHAEOLOGICAL RESOURCES					
15	What is the integrity of known maritime archaeological resources and how is it changing?	▼	Natural deterioration (physical, biological and chemical).	The diminished condition of selected archaeological resources has reduced, to some extent, their historical, scientific or educational value and may affect the eligibility of some sites for listing in the National Register of Historic Places.	Documentation of known sites. Ongoing surveys to identify new sites.
16	Do known maritime archaeological resources pose an environmental hazard and how is this threat changing?	–	No known resources with hazardous cargos.	Known maritime archaeological resources pose few or no environmental threats.	Continued monitoring and exploration to locate potential threats.
17	What are the levels of human activities that may influence maritime archaeological resource quality and how are they changing?	▲	Few instances of resource removal or damage.	Few or no activities occur that are likely to negatively affect maritime archaeological resource integrity.	All activities are regulated by permits; known locations are protected by federal law; outreach and education increasing awareness of importance of protection.

Site History and Resources

The expansive ecosystems of the Northwestern Hawaiian Islands are among the few large-scale, intact, predator-dominated reef ecosystems left in the world, and one of the most remote (Figure 1). The area is comprised of small islands, islets and atolls and a complex array of shallow coral reefs, deepwater slopes, banks, seamounts, and abyssal and pelagic oceanic ecosystems supporting a diversity of marine life, 25 percent of which is endemic to the Hawaiian Archipelago (Eldredge and Miller 1994, Miller and Eldredge 1996, Randall 1992). The coral reefs of the Northwestern Hawaiian Islands are the foundation of an ecosystem that hosts a distinctive assemblage of marine mammals, fish, sea turtles, birds, algae and invertebrates, including species that are rare, threatened, endangered or have special legal protection status. The Census of Coral Reefs (2006) and Northwestern Hawaiian Islands Reef Assessment and Monitoring Program expeditions (between 2000 and 2006) revealed many previously unreported and undescribed species of reef invertebrates and corals, evidence that the reefs within the monument have not been sufficiently explored and surveyed. Additional explorations and analyses are needed to adequately characterize and document rare habitats and species, especially vulnerable endemic species that may require special management (NMSP 2006).

Location

A vast, remote and largely uninhabited marine region, the monument encompasses an area of 139,792 square miles of Pacific Ocean in the northwestern extent of the Hawaiian Archipelago. The monument is comprised of all lands, including emergent and submerged lands and waters of the Northwestern Hawaiian Islands and is approximately 1,382 miles long and 100 miles wide. The area includes the Northwestern Hawaiian Islands Coral Reef Ecosystem Reserve, the Midway Atoll National Wildlife Refuge/Battle of Midway National

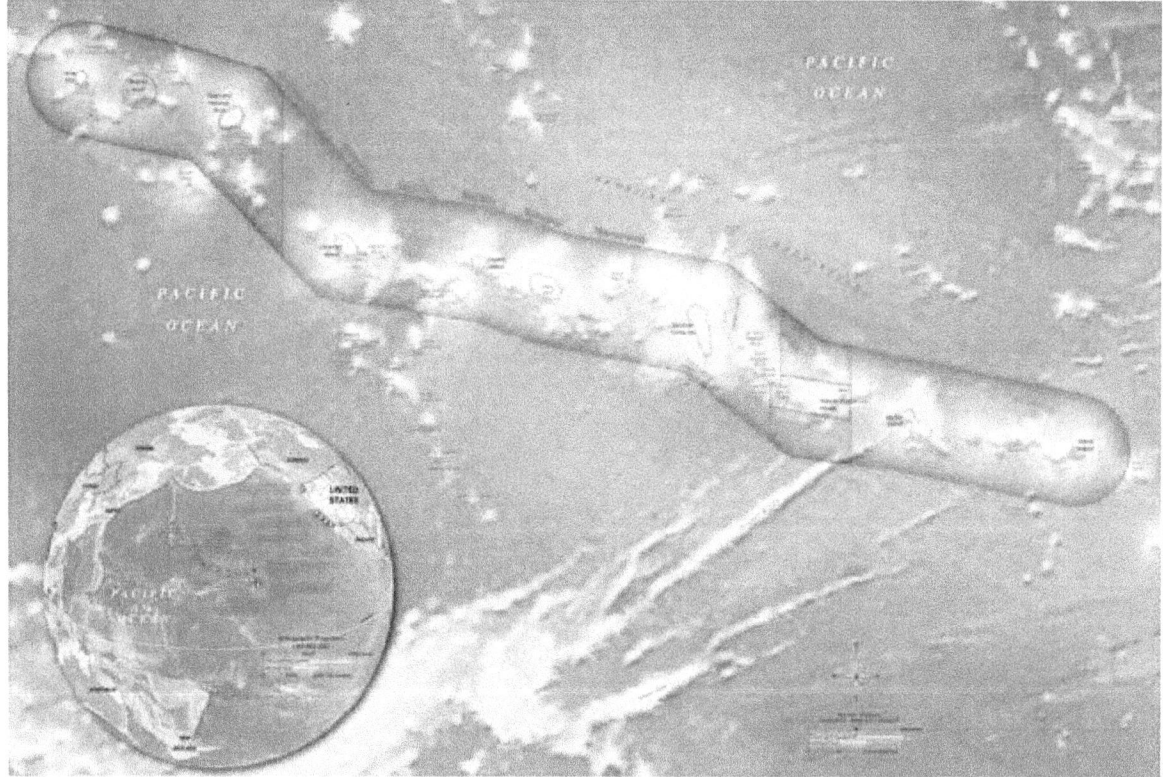

Figure 1. Hawaiian Archipelago including the Northwestern Hawaiian Islands (Nihoa Island to Kure Atoll) and Main Hawaiian Islands (Islands of Hawai'i to Kaua'i). Inset shows the Hawaiian Archipelago in the Pacific Ocean.

Memorial, the Hawaiian Islands National Wildlife Refuge, Kure Atoll Wildlife Sanctuary and the State of Hawaii Northwestern Hawaiian Islands Marine Refuge (71 FR 51134).

Designation

In 2000, the Northwestern Hawaiian Islands Coral Reef Ecosystem Reserve was established by Presidential Executive Order with a mission to carry out coordinated and integrated management to achieve the primary purpose of strong and long-term protection of the marine ecosystems in their natural condition, as well as the perpetuation of Native Hawaiian cultural practices and the conservation of heritage resources of the Northwestern Hawaiian Islands. The Executive Orders that created the reserve in 2000 also initiated a process to designate the waters of the Northwestern Hawaiian Islands as a federal national marine sanctuary. In 2006, after substantial public comment in support of strong protections for the area, President George W. Bush signed a proclamation creating the Northwestern Hawaiian Islands Marine National Monument. The president's actions afforded the Northwestern Hawaiian Islands our nation's highest form of marine environmental protection. Subsequently, through an initiative put forth by the Northwestern Hawaiian Islands Native Hawaiian Cultural Working Group, the monument was given the Hawaiian name, Papahānaumokuākea Marine National Monument, in March 2007. The monument is co-managed by the Department of the Interior's U.S. Fish and Wildlife Service, the Department of Commerce's National Oceanic and Atmospheric Administration (NOAA), and the State of Hawaii, and is now the single largest conservation area under the U.S. flag.

Early Settlement and Discovery

One of the most remarkable feats of open-ocean voyaging and settlement in all of human history was the movement of ancestral Oceanic people across the vast Pacific Ocean. The Northwestern Hawaiian Islands were explored, colonized, and in some cases, permanently settled by Native Hawaiians in pre-contact times. Nihoa and Necker Island (Mokumanamana), the islands closest to the main Hawaiian Islands, have archaeological sites with agricultural, religious and habitation features (Figure 2). Based on radiocarbon data, it has been estimated that Nihoa and Necker Islands could have been inhabited from 1000 A.D. to 1700 A.D. In the Hawaiian Archipelago, the northwestern region contained the most peripheral islands that relied heavily on interaction and networking between core islands (the main Hawaiian Islands) as a social mechanism to help reduce the possibility of extinction of their geographically isolated populations (Emory 1928, Cleghorn 1988).

Though Hawaiian traditions retained the names of a handful of islands in the northwestern chain, regular contact had long ceased by the time Captain Cook's two ships made the first European contact with the Hawaiian islands in 1778. Later, many of the reefs and atolls in the Northwestern Hawaiian Islands were discovered by westerners in the 1800s either intentionally or when ships ran aground. Some of the locations, such as Maro Reef, Laysan Island, and Pearl and Hermes Atoll, received their historic names from the shipwrecked vessels.

Referred to as the Kūpuna (elder) Islands, the Northwestern Hawaiian Islands are ceded lands (crown lands belonging to the Hawaiian monarchy at the time Hawaii was annexed by the United States) and extremely important to the Native Hawaiian people. Their rich

Figure 2. Stones placed several hundred years ago by Polynesian visitors at Mokumanamana, or Necker Island, for spiritual or navigational purposes.

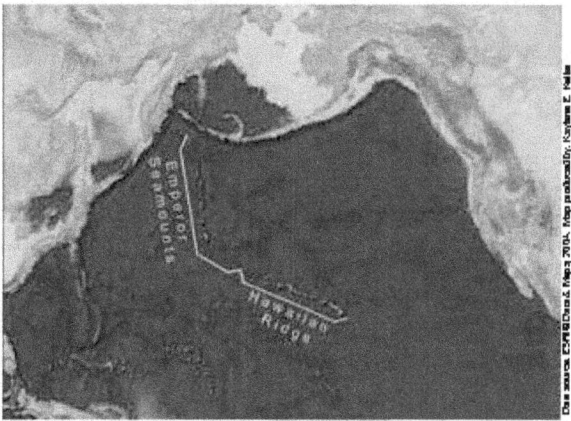

Figure 3. Map of part of the Pacific basin showing the volcanic trail of the Hawaiian hotspot—6,000-km-long Hawaiian Ridge-Emperor Seamounts chain.

cultural resources inform us about the origins of Hawaii's first people and hold great significance in Native Hawaiian culture and history. Myth and culture join in ancient oli (chant) and mele (song) telling of the fire goddess Pele and her family traversing the Northwestern Hawaiian Islands and stopping at Mokumanamana on their way to the main Hawaiian Islands (NMSP 2005).

Geology

Over the past 70 million years or more, the combined processes of magma formation, volcano eruption and growth, and continued movement of the Pacific Plate over a magmatic "hotspot" have left a long trail of volcanoes across the Pacific Ocean floor (Figure 3). The Hawaiian Ridge-Emperor Seamount chain extends 3,728 miles from the "Big Island" of Hawaii to the Aleutian and Kamchatka trenches off Alaska and Siberia respectively. The Hawaiian Islands themselves are a very small part of the chain and are the youngest islands in the immense, mostly submarine mountain chain composed of more than 80 volcanoes (Clague 1996).

A sharp bend in the chain indicates that the motion of the Pacific Plate abruptly changed about 43 million years ago as it took a more westerly turn from its earlier northerly direction. The formation of the bend coincides with a major reorganization of northern Pacific seafloor spreading centers and the initiation of subduction at the Mariana arc-trench system (Sharp and Clague 2006).

As the Pacific Plate continues to move west-northwest, the Island of Hawaii will be carried beyond the hotspot by plate motion, setting the stage for the formation of a new volcanic island in its place (Figure 4). Loihi Seamount, an active submarine volcano, is forming about 22 miles off the southern coast of Hawaii. Loihi already has risen about two miles above the ocean floor to within one mile of the ocean surface. According to the hotspot theory, assuming Loihi continues to grow, it will become the next island in the Hawaiian chain. In the geologic future, Loihi may eventually become fused with the Island of Hawaii, which itself is composed of five volcanoes knitted together: Kohala, Mauna Kea, Hualalai, Mauna Loa and Kilauea.

The Northwestern Hawaiian Islands constitute the northwest three-fourths of the vast chain of the Hawaiian Archipelago. Moving northwest from the main Hawaiian Islands, this stretch of emergent lands is characterized as small rocky islands, banks, atolls, coral islands and reefs, which become progressively older moving from east to west. The reefs are some of the healthiest and least disturbed coral reefs remaining and make up one of the very last large-scale, predator-dominated coral reef ecosystem on the planet. Over millennia, invertebrate animals and algae have constructed massive reefs

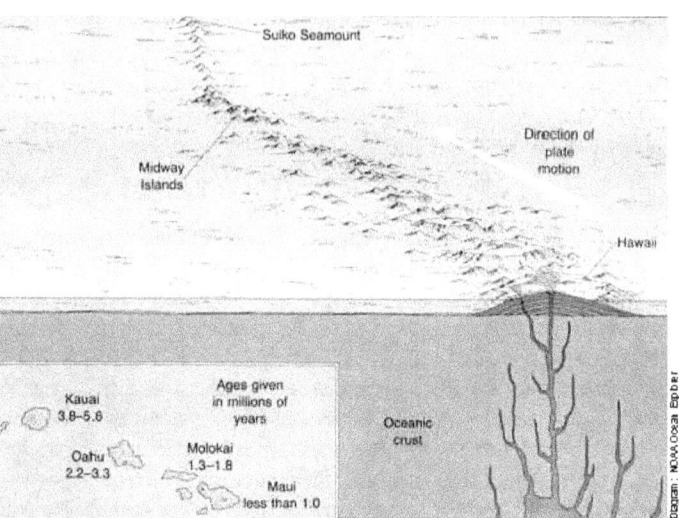

Figure 4. The Pacific plate slowly moves over the Hawaiian hotspot to the northwest at an average rate of 9.5 cm/yr. Kure atoll, the most northern emergent land, was formed approximately 30 million years ago (Wessel et al. 2006). The area directly over the hotspot is volcanically active. The activity decreases and eventually stops as the plate moves on.

in the shallow seas surrounding the islands. Coral animals and coralline algae, initially attached to the basalt of the ancient volcanoes, accreted gradually by secreting skeletons of calcium carbonate. The basaltic islands eventually eroded away and subsided under their own massive weight. However, the upward growth of the coral reefs has kept pace with the gradual sinking of the volcanic remnants, leaving the reefs we see today.

Due to the remote locale of the reefs of the Northwestern Hawaiian Islands dispersal and recruitment of reef species from the rest of the Pacific is an uncommon event. Long periods of isolation for the survivors led to the evolution of species distinct from those that evolved independently on the host reefs, resulting in the highest levels of marine endemism recorded for a large archipelago in the world (Randall 1992, Eldredge and Miller 1994, Miller and Eldredge 1996). Surveys and explorations to date have yet to adequately characterize the actual degree of endemism in the Northwestern Hawaiian Islands, especially for reef invertebrates, corals and algae (NMSP 2005).

Water: Oceanographic Conditions

Ocean currents transport and distribute larvae among and between different atolls, islands and submerged banks of the Northwestern Hawaiian Islands and also provide the mechanism by which species are distributed to and from the main Hawaiian Islands, as well as far distant regions. Upper ocean currents in the Northwestern

Hawaiian Islands are highly variable in both speed and direction, being dominated by eddy variability. Averaged over time, the resultant mean flow of the surface waters tends to flow predominantly from east to west in response to the prevailing northeast tradewinds (Firing et al. 2004).

Significant wave events vary over interannual (between year) and decadal time scales, which can also determine distributions of species of corals and algae and their associated fish and invertebrate assemblages. Interannually, some years experience greater or lesser amounts of cumulative wave energy or numbers of extreme wave events than other years (Figure 5). This apparent decadal variability of wave power is possibly related to well-documented Pacific Decadal Oscillation events, which are a mode of North Pacific climate variability at multi-decadal time scales that has widespread climate and ecosystem impacts (Mantua et al. 1997).

The coral reefs of the Northwestern Hawaiian Islands, particularly Kure, Midway, and Pearl and Hermes Atolls at the northwestern end of the archipelago, are exposed to large seasonal temperature fluctuations. Sea surface temperatures at these northerly atolls range from less than 18°C in late winter of some years (17°C in 1997) to highs exceeding 28°C in the late summer months of some years (29°C in 2002). Compared with most reef ecosystems around the globe, these fluctuations are extremely high. While the summer temperatures are generally similar along the entire Northwestern Hawaiian Islands chain, the winter temperatures tend to be 3-7°C cooler

at the northerly atolls than at the southerly islands and banks as the subtropical front migrates southward.

Satellite observations reveal a significant chlorophyll front associated with the subtropical front, with high chlorophyll north of the front and oligotrophic waters south of the front. These observations reveal significant seasonal and interannual migrations of the front northward during the summer months and southward during the winter months (Seki et al. 2002). The southward migration of the subtropical front generally brings these high-chlorophyll waters into the northern portions of the Northwestern Hawaiian Islands. During some years, these winter migrations of the subtropical front extend southward to include the southern end of the Northwestern Hawaiian Islands. Additional evidence suggests decadal scale movements in the southward extent of the subtropical front (Friedlander et al. 2005).

Habitat

The monument is comprised of a complex array of reef, slope, bank, seamount, abyssal and pelagic marine environments. The healthy and extensive shallow-water coral reefs encompass over 4,450 square miles of shallow-water coral reef habitat. Pearl and Hermes Atoll, French Frigate Shoals, Maro Reef, and Lisianski Island have the most extensive near-shore reefs (Figure 6). Gardner Pinnacles, Lisianski Island, Maro Reef and Necker Island have the most extensive shallow-water bank areas (NOAA 1998).

Within the Northwestern Hawaiian Islands, the reefs differ in coral cover and species organization. This vast, shallow-water coral reef ecosystem supports a dynamic system of marine species. Up to 25 percent of the shallow-water organisms found in the Hawaiian Islands are endemic, or are found nowhere else on earth. It has been hypothesized that the Northwestern Hawaiian Islands act as stepping stones

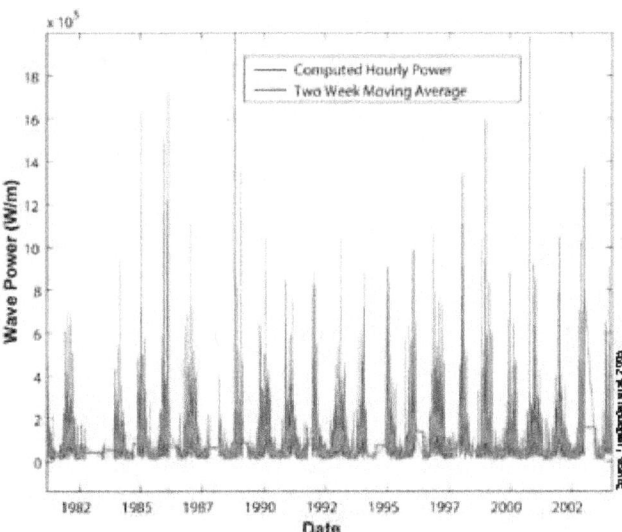

Figure 5. Time series of wave power computed from wave data from NOAA Buoy #51001 located near Nihoa Island in the Northwestern Hawaiian Islands. Data courtesy of NOAA Data Buoy Center.

Figure 6. Table corals, such as these *Acropora* are common throughout the tropical Pacific and at French Frigate Shoals, but absent in the main Hawaiian Islands.

and reservoirs for organisms found in the main Hawaiian Islands, just as their predecessors in the Emperor Seamounts may have served as the stepping stones for the Northwestern Hawaiian Islands (NOS 2003).

The monument is also comprised of a unique system of terrestrial environments, which will be mentioned but not expanded upon in this report. Many of the Northwestern Hawaiian Islands islets and atolls have been relatively untouched by humans. Nihoa Island is one of the most biologically pristine islands in the Pacific and probably most closely represents the original island appearance and native species found before humans arrived in the Hawaiian Islands, although recent infestations of alien grasshoppers periodically threaten the vegetation and other terrestrial wildlife. Many of the islands provide breeding sites for numerous central Pacific seabirds that nest in burrows and cliffs, on the ground, and in trees and shrubs. For some species, these tiny specks of land provide their only breeding sites.

Figure 7. The Hawaiian monk seal is the second most endangered marine mammal in the world, after its close relative, the Mediterranean monk seal.

Living Resources

The coral reefs of the Northwestern Hawaiian Islands are inhabited by at least 57 species of coral species, 355 algae species and many invertebrate species. Thorough and systematic explorations will likely add to these numbers. This diversity and species richness now exceeds that of the main Hawaiian Islands. Indeed, the Northwestern Hawaiian Islands host an exceptionally high number of endemic corals and algae (Maragos et al. 2004).

The Northwestern Hawaiian Islands ecosystems play an important role in supporting a host of marine mammals. Hawaiian monk seals (Figure 7), and Hawaiian spinner and bottlenose dolphins are resident species that occur within these ecosystems during the entire year. Transient species such as spotted dolphins, humpback whales and numerous other cetaceans occur seasonally within the monument.

The endemic Hawaiian monk seal, the most endangered marine mammal in the United States, is the only seal dependent upon coral reefs for its existence. The first range-wide beach counts of monk seals occurred in the late 1950s. Due to a 50 percent decline discovered in beach counts, the Hawaiian monk seal was listed as endangered throughout its range in 1976. NOAA Fisheries designated critical habitat for the Hawaiian monk seal from shore out to 20 fathoms throughout the Northwestern Hawaiian Islands in May 1988. Since that time additional research has indicated that the seals also forage in very deep waters on offshore banks and seamounts (Parrish et al. 2002). In recent years the seal population has continued to decline. Beach counts are used as an index of the population, and in 2008 the

mean number of seals older than pups observed in beach counts at the six major NWHI subpopulations was a little over 300 seals (NMFS unpublished data). An estimated 1,100 to 1,200 animals remain throughout the island chain (Carretta et al. 2008).

The Northwestern Hawaiian Islands are an important nesting habitat for the threatened green sea turtle, which occupies three habitat types: open beaches, open sea and shallow, protected waters (Figure 8). Eastern Island at French Frigate Shoals alone accounts for more than 80 percent of the nesting population for the entire archipelago. Upon hatching, the young turtles crawl from the beach and swim over shallow reef areas and extensive shoal areas to the open ocean. When their shells grow 8 to 10 inches long, they move to shallow feeding grounds over coral reefs and rocky bottoms. Age at sexual maturity is estimated at 20 to 50 years. While the green sea turtle is a resident species, the endangered leatherback, the endangered olive ridley, and the threatened loggerhead sea turtles are considered transient species that occur seasonally in this expansive area. The endangered hawksbill turtle is also a resident in Hawaii, with small nesting populations near the southeast end of the archipelago and with feeding populations throughout the islands.

The Northwestern Hawaiian Islands support some unique species of marine life that are also found in geographically distant ecosystems. It is believed that the Northwestern Hawaiian Islands are linked to these ecosystems via associated seamounts and the island groups adjacent to them. Some of these unique fish species commonly

Figure 8. Green sea turtles are found around most of the islands in the Hawaiian Archipelago. Their primary nesting site is at French Frigate Shoals.

Figure 9. Bow of the USS Macaw ASR-11, which was a 250-foot salvage and rescue ship. During salvage operations in 1944, the Macaw ran aground and subsequently sank during a powerful storm.

found on the reefs in the monument, such as the slingjaw wrasse, the masked angelfish and the knifejaw are rare elsewhere in the Hawaiian archipelago. The total number of species in the Northwest Hawaiian Islands is unknown, but initial sampling indicates the presence of approximately 260 fish species at Midway alone (Randall 1992).

Structurally, apex predators, such as sharks and jacks, dominate fish communities on the reefs. In addition, abundance and biomass estimates indicate that the reef community is characterized by fewer herbivores, such as surgeonfishes, and more carnivores, such as damselfishes, goatfishes and scorpionfishes. The value of these exquisite reef communities extends beyond the intrinsic; they also have the potential to hedge against fisheries collapses in the main Hawaiian Islands by potentially serving as a source of recruits and propagules.

The Northwestern Hawaiian Islands are home to millions of seabirds and the largest seabird rookery under unified management in the Pacific. Four endangered endemic bird species, Laysan duck, Laysan finch, Nihoa finch and Nihoa millerbird, breed on the islands along with approximately 14 million seabirds of 22 species.

The coral reefs of the Northwestern Hawaiian Islands support diverse communities of benthic macroinvertebrates. Mollusks, crustaceans and echinoderms dominate the non-coral invertebrate fauna in the Northwestern Hawaiian Islands, which is typical for most coral reef communities. As many as 600 species of macroinvertebrates were identified at French Frigate Shoals alone on the 2000 Northwestern Hawaiian Islands Reef Assessment and Monitoring Program expedi-

tion, with more than 250 species (not including marine snails) reported as new records. In October 2006, a Census of Coral Reefs (2006) expedition to French Frigate Shoals returned with numerous species that have yet to be identified. More than 100 new species records are expected from this expedition (NMSP 2005, Friedlander et al. 2005).

Maritime Archaeological Resources

The Hawaiian Islands have a rich maritime history (Figure 9). During the late 18th and early 19th centuries, European and American traders began to call at the main Hawaiian Islands, and by 1825, Honolulu became the most important port in the Pacific. During the 19th and 20th centuries, the Northwestern Hawaiian Islands experienced a series of extractive activities, including fishing, guano mining, shipwreck salvage cruises, bird poaching (feathers), and pearl oyster collection, as well as commercial exploitation of other marine and terrestrial wildlife. The geographic location of the Northwestern Hawaiian Islands became increasingly important to commercial and military planners. The opening of the Japan Whaling grounds in 1820 sent ships through the Northwestern Hawaiian Islands in pursuit of whale oil. Midway was claimed by the U.S. government in 1867 and by the turn of the century had become an important transpacific cable station and stopping point for the flying "Clippers" carrying passengers and mail between San Francisco and Manila. In 1940, the U.S. Navy constructed the Pacific Naval Air Base, and subsequently a submarine base, at Midway. During World War II, patrol vessels were stationed at most of the islands and atolls.

Figure 10. *Archaeological evidence of human habitation on Nihoa. Also in photo is a red-footed boobie.*

The Northwestern Hawaiian Islands have been a veritable grave-yard of marine disaster. The low, inconspicuous character of the islands and their faulty or insufficient location on marine charts, in conjunction with the numerous activities that have occurred over the past few centuries have left a scattered maritime legacy around and on the islands, including shipwrecks and sunken naval aircraft. Currently, there are 60 known shipwreck sites among the Northwestern Hawaiian Islands. The earliest sites discovered so far include the whaling ships Pearl and Hermes dating back to 1822. Combined with known aircraft, there are a total of 127 known potential maritime resource sites (Van Tilburg 2002). Twenty of these sites have been confirmed by field survey including five 19th century whaling ships, which represent an important period of whaling history in the Pacific. Many of these heritage resources, as defined by State and Federal Preservation Laws, are of historical and national significance. Some of these ship and aircraft wreck sites fall into the category of war graves associated with major historic events, such as the Battle of Midway in June 1942. They are a physical record of past activities in the Northwestern Hawaiian Islands and embody unique aspects of Island and Pacific history.

Native Hawaiian Cultural Resources

Indigenous Hawaiians have a connection to and interest in the Northwestern Hawaiian Islands, which is documented in their oral and written histories, genealogies, spirituality, songs and dance. Polynesians traveled thousands of miles over hundreds of years in the Northwestern Hawaiian Islands and there is archaeological evidence of human habitation on Nihoa over a period of 500 to 700 years (Figure 10). There are also recorded visits to these islands by the monarchs of the Hawaiian Nation, which extended out to the Northwestern Hawaiian Islands.

In Hawaiian traditions, the Northwestern Hawaiian Islands are considered a sacred place, a region of primordial darkness from which life springs and spirits return after death (Kikiloi 2006). According to Hawaiian traditional practices, in which responsibilities are inherited from ancestors, ancestral deities, and a multitude of gods, and also in accordance with perpetual indigenous Hawaiian sovereign authority, indigenous people of Hawaii have inherited inalienable duties to care for and protect the "body forms" that preceded them in the evolutionary process. These body forms include coral polyps, seaweed, fish, all other ocean life forms, birds, and islands. Connections to these body forms are genealogically based. They are all ancestors, connected to the Hawaiian people in space, time and spiritual energy. Therefore, indigenous people of Hawaii have the responsibility to honor and protect their ancestors who reside in the Northwestern Hawaiian Islands in their multitude of forms (NMSP 2005).

Pressures on the Monument

Numerous human activities and natural events and processes affect the condition of natural and archaeological resources in marine environments. This section describes the nature and extent of the most prominent pressures on the monument.

Marine Pollution
Marine Debris

Many reefs in the Northwestern Hawaiian Islands and throughout the Pacific have been inundated with large amounts of debris lost by North Pacific commercial fishing operations or dispersed from other marine or terrestrial sources. These objects degrade reef health by abrading, poisoning, smothering and dislodging corals and other benthic organisms, and entangling fish, marine mammals, crustaceans and other mobile species. Marine debris containing hazardous materials such as pesticides, petroleum, toxic chemicals and phosphorus flares washes up on the beaches of the Northwestern Hawaiian Islands and is a danger to wildlife and humans. It is unknown how much of these toxic compounds are released from the debris while floating in the marine environment. Marine debris and derelict fishing gear hinder the recovery of the critically endangered Hawaiian monk seal and threatened sea turtles through entanglement, drowning and suffocation (NMSP 2005).

The North Pacific Subtropical Convergence Zone provides a mechanism for derelict fishing gear and other marine debris either lost or discarded throughout the Pacific Rim to accumulate in the Northwestern Hawaiian Islands (Figure 11). Under certain conditions, this convergence zone moves to encompass the Northwestern Hawaiian Islands and deposits tons of net and line on these shallow reef systems. Derelict gear may circulate for years in ocean gyres and currents until it snags on a shoal. The extensive shallow reefs of the Northwestern Hawaiian Islands are ideal for such debris settlement. Once derelict gear catches on organisms of the remote reefs and atolls of the Northwestern Hawaiian Islands, it begins a process of destructive activity.

Coastal and Terrestrial Pollution

Past uses of the Northwestern Hawaiian Islands have left a legacy of contamination on many of the atolls. The Northwestern Hawaiian Islands have hosted an array of polluting human activities including guano mining, fishing camps, U.S. Coast Guard LORAN stations, various Cold War military missions, and U.S. Navy airfields and bases (Figure 12). Contamination at all these sites includes onshore and offshore debris such as batteries (lead and mercury), PCB-containing transformers, capacitors, and barrels of petroleum and other chemicals. Many of the common contaminants biomagnify so that small amounts found in sediment can result in significant concentrations in upper trophic levels.

Several areas of contamination have been identified in the Northwestern Hawaiian Islands and include the following (Friedlander et al. 2005):

■ Kure and French Frigate Shoals both have point sources of PCBs due to former U.S. Coast Guard LORAN stations. While the U.S. Coast Guard has mounted limited cleanup actions at both sites, contamination remains and is found in island soils and in nearshore sediments and biota.

Figure 11. Derelict fishing gear at Midway Atoll.

Figure 12. Sand (forefront) and Eastern Islands at Midway Atoll, the site of a U.S. naval air facility during the World War II and Cold War eras, before Midway was transferred to the U.S. Fish and Wildlife Service in 1996.

■ Tern Island, a part of the French Frigate Shoals atoll, was formed into a runway to serve as a refueling stop for planes enroute to Midway during World War II and served as the site of various Cold War missions. Leaking underground storage tanks were a source of petroleum contamination until removed by the Army Corps of Engineers.

■ The U.S. Navy built a naval air facility and submarine base at Midway Atoll and during base reduction and closure identified and cleaned up numerous sites contaminated with petroleum, pesticides, PCBs and metals. While most known areas were remediated, several areas, including unlined eroding landfills, warrant continued monitoring for potential releases.

■ Plutonium from the aboveground nuclear tests in the 1960s at Johnston Atoll has been detected in corals 700 miles to the north at French Frigate Shoals.

Climate Change and Coral Bleaching

Climatic events play an important role in the ecosystem productivity of the Northwestern Hawaiian Islands. Fluctuations in the abundances of monk seals, reef fishes and chlorophyll have been documented from the early 1980s to the present and may be associated with multidecadal climate oscillations. While severe tropical storms or typhoons are rare, winter storms are common, resulting in a noticeable increase in winds and high seas that impact the reef system.

Problems associated with increased sea surface temperatures have been reported in the Northwestern Hawaiian Islands. Sea surface temperature information obtained from NOAA demonstrated that water temperatures at Midway rose nearly two degrees centigrade over the usual summer maxima in August of 2002. Corresponding with this warm water event, substantial coral bleaching was observed—a process whereby coral colonies lose their color due to the expulsion of symbiotic microscopic algae (zooxanthellae) from most coral tissues—on reefs at the three northwestern most atolls: Kure, Midway, and Pearl and Hermes (Figure 13). At the three northern atolls, bleaching was most severe on the backreef, moderate in the lagoon, and low on the deeper forereef (Kenyon et al. 2006). No significant bleaching was found the following year during surveys conducted in July 2003. Substantial coral bleaching at several reef systems was confirmed in the Northwestern Hawaiian Islands during surveys conducted in September and October 2004 (Kenyon and Brainard 2006). Military construction, including the dredging of a ship channel and filling for the airfields, dramatically changed water levels and circulation in the Midway lagoon, and may have exacerbated the effects of 2002 and 2004 lagoon coral bleaching. At Pearl and Hermes Atoll and Midway Atoll, bleaching was most pronounced in the shallow backreef habitat. The incidence of bleaching

Figure 13. Partially bleached *Porites* sp. coral in the monument.

in the shallow backreef habitat at Kure, the northernmost atoll in the Hawaiian Archipelago, was less than that at Pearl and Hermes and at Midway (NMSP 2005, Friedlander et al. 2005, Hoeke et al. 2006)

Climate models predict that global average sea level may rise considerably this century, potentially affecting species that rely on coastal habitat. Most of the Northwestern Hawaiian Islands are low lying and therefore potentially vulnerable to increases in global average sea level. The effects of habitat loss on Northwestern Hawaiian Islands biota are difficult to predict, but may be greatest for endangered Hawaiian monk seals and threatened Hawaiian green sea turtles at Pearl and Hermes Reef (Baker et al. 2006).

Diseases

There has been a worldwide increase in the reports of diseases affecting marine organisms. However, the factors contributing to disease outbreaks are poorly understood due to lack of information on normal disease levels in the ocean. The Northwestern Hawaiian Islands are considered to be one of the last relatively pristine large coral reef ecosystems remaining in the world. As such, it provides the unique opportunity to document what may be the normal levels of disease in a coral reef system exposed to limited human influence (Friedlander et al. 2005, Harvell et al. 1999).

Recent studies in the Northwestern Hawaiian Islands have begun to document baseline levels of coral and fish disease (Work et al. 2004, Aeby 2006) (http://www.hawaii.edu/HIMB/HawaiiCoralDisease/) (Figure 14). Tumors, as well as lesions associated with parasites, ciliates, bacteria and fungi, have been found on a number of coral species. During a 2003 survey of 73 sites throughout the Northwestern Hawaiian Islands, evidence of coral disease was found at very low levels at 68.5 percent of the sites across all regions. The

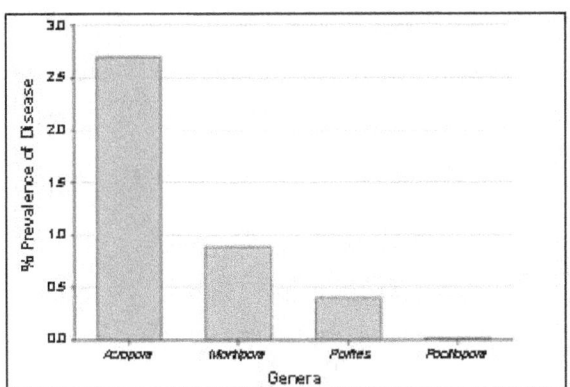

Figure 14. Differences in overall prevalence of disease among coral genera in the Northwestern Hawaiian Islands.

overall average prevalence of disease (number of diseased colonies/ total number of colonies) was estimated at 0.5 percent (range 0-7.1 percent) compared to the average prevalence of disease of 0.95 percent in the main Hawaiian Islands. The prevalence of disease varies among different genera of coral with the highest prevalence in species of the genera Porites and Acropora. Recent disease observed on giant table corals at French Frigate Shoals may have spread from Johnston Atoll about 520 miles to the south (Friedlander et al. 2005).

In the Hawaiian Archipelago, more than 50 percent of endangered Hawaiian green sea turtles nest at East Island, French Frigate Shoals in the Northwestern Hawaiian Islands. Green sea turtles are affected by fibropapillomatosis, a disease that causes tumors in turtles. Although most cases of the disease in the Hawaiian Islands have been observed in the main Hawaiian Islands, green sea turtles are highly migratory. The prevalence of fibropapillomatosis in the Hawaiian green turtle population was estimated at 40 to 60 percent, with the majority of cases found among juvenile turtles. The majority of recent turtle strandings are by juvenile turtles with the disease (Work et al. 2004). As such, fibropapillomatosis may pose a significant threat to the long-term survival of the species (Quackenbush et al. 2001, NMFS and USFWS 1998).

Alien Species

Alien species can be defined as organisms that are not native to a particular ecosystem and have been accidentally or deliberately introduced to an area outside of their historic geographic range. An invasive species is one that demonstrates rapid growth and spread, invades habitats, and displaces native organisms. A total of 11 introduced invertebrate, fish and algal species have been recorded in the Northwestern Hawaiian Islands and are generally low in number and impact. One potential exception to this is the coral disease observed on table coral which has an unknown source and may possibly be caused by an alien (introduced) species. Alien species may be introduced unintentionally by vessels, marine debris or aquaculture, or intentionally, as in the case of some species of groupers, snappers and algae. Eleven species of shallow-water snappers and groupers were purposely introduced to one or more of the main Hawaiian Islands in the late 1950s (Randall 1987). Presently, two of these introduced fish, the ta'ape (Lutajanus kasmira) and the roi (Cephalopholis argus) are now established in the Northwestern Hawaiian Islands.

Populations of alien marine species that have already colonized areas of the main Hawaiian Islands represent the most likely source of invasive species in the Northwestern Hawaiian Islands. Most can be found from littoral zones to deep water coral beds. The few alien species known from the Northwestern Hawaiian Islands are mostly restricted to areas of higher human activity at Midway Atoll and French Frigate Shoals (Godwin et al. 2005).

Though not all introduced species will become invasive, those that do could have some of the following potential environmental impacts to the Northwestern Hawaiian Islands (State of Hawaii 2003):

- loss of native biodiversity;

- functional changes of freshwater, other inland waters, and near-shore marine ecosystems;

- alterations in nutrient cycling pathways; and

- decreased water quality.

Fishing

Between 1750 and the 1920s, western explorers harvested monk seals, whales, fish, seabirds and guano from various parts of the Northwestern Hawaiian Islands. More recently, the history of fishing and other resource extractive uses included the overexploitation of the indigenous black-lipped pearl oyster (1928 to 1930), the beginning of a commercial fishing fleet (1930s to 1940s), a cessation of commercial uses during World War II, a resumption of commercial fishing (1945 to 1960) during which Tern Island was used as a trans-shipment point for fresh fish flown to Honolulu, and a proliferation of foreign fishing vessels from Japan to Russia (1965 to 1977). Currently fishery management plans exist for precious corals, bottomfish, pelagics, crustaceans and coral reef fisheries, however, the only active fishery is for bottomfish.

The recent Presidential Proclamation that established the monument determined that commercial fishing for bottomfish and associated pelagic species may continue within the monument until June 15, 2011. The proclamation established caps for total landings for each fishing year at 350,000 pounds for bottomfish species and 180,000 pounds for

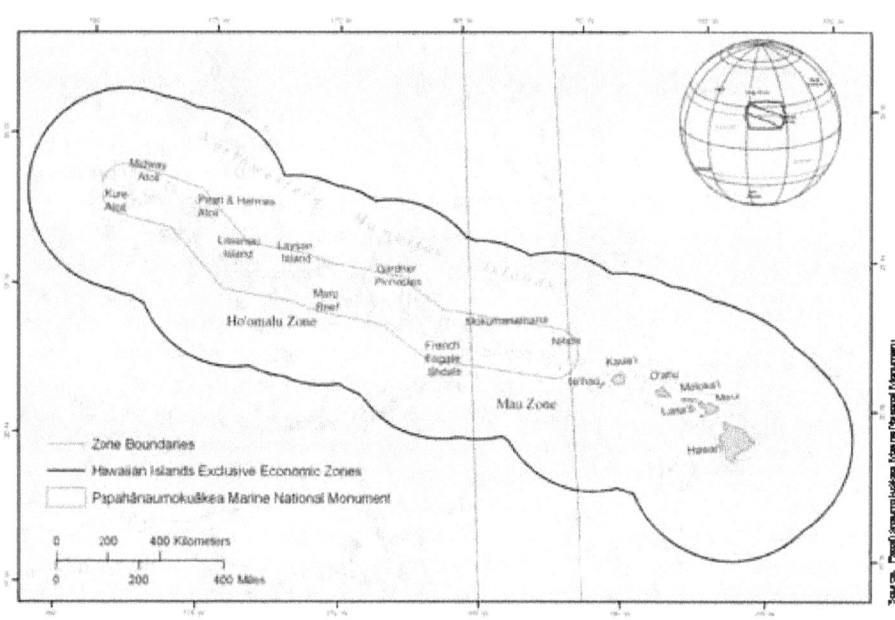

Figure 15. Bottomfish fisheries are divided into management subareas in the Hawaiian Archipelago. As of 2003, five bottomfish vessels operate in the Mau Zone, and four operate in the Ho'omalu Zone.

pelagic species. After June 15, 2011, commercial fishing for bottomfish and associated pelagic species will be prohibited in the monument.

Commercial Bottomfish

The federally permitted Northwestern Hawaiian Islands commercial bottomfish fishery has been regulated under the current management regime since 1986 (Figure 15). The fishery targets deepwater (generally > 75-100 fm) snappers, and one endemic species of grouper (WPRFMC 2004). The allowable gear and fishing requirements were designed to minimize habitat impacts and maintain by-catch levels of approximately 25 percent (WPRFMC 1986, NMSP 2004b).

Fishing effort in the main Hawaiian Islands is the major stress on the bottomfish fishery in the Hawaiian archipelago. However, in 2002, data suggested that fishing effort had exceeded acceptable levels in the Mau zone, one of two fishing zones established in the Northwestern Hawaiian Islands. Data from the following year indicated that overfishing was no longer occurring in the Mau zone, and currently there is no reason to believe that the fishing mortality metrics for either of the Northwestern Hawaiian Islands' zones (Mau or Ho'omalu) will change significantly in the future. Nonetheless, it has been recognized that the assessment methods rely heavily on fishery-dependent data sets that lack information on important segments of the population. As such, a Bottomfish Stock Assessment Panel was convened by the Western Pacific Regional Fishery Management Council in January 2004 to develop a plan to improve data collection and assessment methodologies (NMSP 2004b).

Commercial Pelagic Fisheries

TROLLING

A very small number of commercial pelagic trolling fishermen have recently operated in the Northwestern Hawaiian Islands. These fishermen do not have federal fishing permits, as the fishery management plan for pelagic species does not regulate this small fleet. The fishermen operated under a State of Hawaii commercial marine license that enabled them to sell their catch legally.

Hawaii's commercial pelagic fishery is divided into four distinct types of fisheries: pole and line (aku) boats, handline (ika shibi and palu ahi) boats, pelagic trolling boats, and pelagic longline (swordfish and tuna) boats. Of these, pelagic trolling is the most popular statewide, with 90 percent of the participants and 50 percent of the small boat landings (WPRFMC 2003). The Hawaii Department of Land and Natural Resources, Division of Aquatic Resources has records for nine commercial pelagic trolling vessels fishing in the Northwestern Hawaiian Islands between 1991 and 2000. The current fishing gear and methods have little to no impact on the habitat and have very low levels of bycatch. However, activities associated with fishing vessels, such as anchoring, could damage submerged historic shipwreck and aircraft sites (NMSP 2004b).

LONGLINING

Commercial pelagic longlining was prohibited within 50 nautical miles of the Northwestern Hawaiian Islands in 1991 because of interactions with endangered and threatened species within the Protected Species Zone.

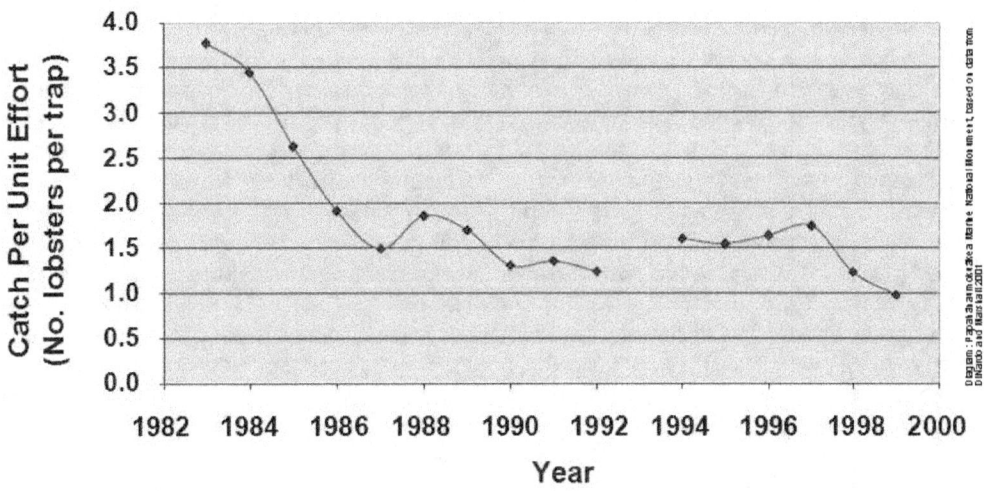

Figure 16. Commercial Lobster Catch Per Unit Effort (all species) in the Northwestern Hawaiian Islands.

Commercial Lobster Fishery

The now-closed, commercial lobster fishery began in 1976 (Figure 16). Advances in trap design and processing techniques led to a steady increase in total landings. Catch per unit effort (lobsters per trap) declined dramatically between 1983 and 1987. In 1991, NOAA Fisheries issued an emergency closure of the fishery. Reasons for closure included: (1) a decrease in catch per unit effort below acceptable levels; (2) indications of sporadic or poor recruitment events; and (3) an indication that the spawning stock biomass was at 22 percent of pre-exploitation levels, which was close to the 20 percent definition of overfishing (NMSP 2004b).

The Northwestern Hawaiian Islands lobster fishery was closed in 2000 by both federal court order related to the National Environmental Policy Act and protected species issues, and by NOAA Fisheries to protect lobster stocks because of: (1) shortcomings in understanding the dynamics of the Northwestern Hawaiian Islands lobster populations; (2) uncertainty in population model parameter estimates; and (3) the lack of appreciable rebuilding of the lobster population despite significant reductions in fishing effort throughout the Northwestern Hawaiian Islands. Additionally, there was some concern at the time that the lobster fishery could impact juvenile monk seal foraging success. However, dietary studies of monk seals have been inconclusive because they were initiated too late to assess the extent to which adult seals or pups forage for lobsters. The Presidential Proclamation of the Northwestern Hawaiian Islands as a marine national monument has determined that any commercial lobster fishing permit shall be subject to a zero annual harvest, which effectively closes the lobster fishery in perpetuity (NMSP 2004b).

Recreational and Sport Fishing Activities

Recreational catch and keep fishing is prohibited in the monument. Recreational fishing had previously taken place in the vicinity of Nihoa Island, based on reports of pelagic spearfishing and recreational trolling by fishermen from the main Hawaiian Islands. Catch and effort data is unavailable for this fishing activity.

Historical Trade in Coral and Reef Species

The harvest of live rock and live coral is currently prohibited throughout the Hawaiian Archipelago by both state and federal regulations (WPRFMC 2001). The harvest of other coral reef species has been prohibited in federal waters of the Northwestern Hawaiian Islands since the establishment of the Northwestern Hawaiian Islands Coral Reef Ecosystem Reserve in 2000 by Executive Order.

No domestic or commercial precious coral fishery has ever operated in the Northwestern Hawaiian Islands, although a fishery management plan was issued in 1981. One permit was issued to harvest coral under an experimental fishing permit, but the venture was unsuccessful. Although harvest of coral reef species such as black-lipped pearl oysters (Figure 17), turtles and reef fish occurred in the early and mid-1900s, coral reef species are no longer commercially harvested in the Northwestern Hawaiian Islands (NMSP 2004b).

Other Fishing Activities

A short-lived commercial fishing operation involving a single vessel using bottom longlines to catch sharks was conducted at French Frigate Shoals and nearby banks in the year 2000. During one 21-day fishing trip, this vessel caught 990 sharks in the Northwestern Hawaiian Islands consisting mainly of sand-bar sharks at 69 percent, Galapagos sharks at 18 percent, and tiger sharks at 10 percent (Vatter 2003).

Recreational fishing and Native Hawaiian sustenance fishing previously had been at low levels. Sustenance fishing included fishing for pelagic reef and bottomfish species using trolling, handline, and pole and line fishing techniques. Sustenance fishing has taken place aboard research, U.S. Coast Guard and military vessels. This type of fishing is also believed to occur from transiting vessels, including sailboats, although no data exists to confirm this assumption. Fishing effort and landings are currently undocumented, but efforts have been made to collect this information from NOAA ships. NOAA conducted a pilot sustenance fishing survey on all NOAA permitted vessels in 2005-2006. Voluntary reporting indicated that very few fish were caught during the time surveyed. The Presidential Proclamation allows for sustenance fishing and defines it as fishing for bottomfish or pelagic species in which all catch is consumed within the monument, and that is incidental to an activity permitted by the monument. Some illegal foreign fishing activities have also been known to occur around the Northwestern Hawaiian Islands. Regulations are enforced primarily by the U.S. Coast Guard, but enforcement is difficult primarily due to the size of the monument.

Vessel Hazards and Groundings

Hazards to shipping and other forms of maritime traffic are inherent in the Northwestern Hawaiian Islands' 1,200 miles of islands, islets, shallow submerged reefs and shoals. The region is exposed to open ocean weather and sea conditions all year, punctuated by severe winter storm and wave events. Vessel groundings and the release of fuel, cargo, rats and other items pose real threats to the Northwestern Hawaiian Islands. The region contains 127 known potential maritime resource sites. Some represent environmental threats, while others consist chiefly of marine debris and are of little specific value. Wrecks of historic sailing vessels in high energy environments are considered artifact "scatter sites," and do not pose an immediate or critical threat to their surroundings. More modern shipwrecks, such as the fishing vessels *Hoei Maru #5* and *Paradise Queen II* at Kure, or the tanker *Mission San Miguel* at Maro Reef, are greater threats to reef ecosystems. Mechanical damage from the initial grounding, subsequent redeposition of wreck material by storm surge, fishing gear damage to reef and species, and fuel, oil or hazardous contents are all issues to be considered. In some cases it may be more detrimental to remove the grounded vessel than to leave it where it is, and this option must be weighed when deciding how to respond to these threats.

In 1998, the *Paradise Queen II* ran aground at Kure Atoll, spilling 11,000 gallons of diesel fuel and 500 gallons of hydraulic fluids and oil. The vessel also lost 3,000 pounds of frozen lobster tails, 4,000 pounds of bait, 11 miles of lobster pot mainline, and 1,040 lead-weighted plastic lobster traps. Traps rolling around in the surf broke coral and coralline algal structures. In 2000, researchers found broken coral, 600 lobster traps, and the bodies of two monk seals among piles of nets surrounding the decaying wheelhouse (USFWS 2000). Also in 2000, the 85-foot longliner *Swordman I*, carrying more than 6,000 gallons of diesel fuel and hydraulic oil, ran aground at Pearl and Hermes Reef in 2000. Vessel Monitoring System technology allowed agents to track the disaster and quickly send out equipment for a clean-up, costs for which the government had to sue to recover. Since 1976, at least 15 vessels have run aground in the Northwestern Hawaiian Islands. Among these are two recent incidences: the *MN Casitas* (Figure 18) was engaged in marine debris removal when it ran aground at Pearl and Hermes Reef, and the *SN Grendel* is thought to have been adrift without a pilot when it landed on the reef at Kure atoll (NMSP 2005, Friedlander et al. 2005).

Figure 17. Black-lipped pearl oysters, at one time very common, were harvested in the late 1920s to make buttons from their shells.

Figure 18. *MN Casitas* aground at Pearl and Hermes Reef, July 2005.

Tourism and Recreation

Due to the Northwestern Hawaiian Islands' isolation, tourism and recreational activities have historically been extremely limited. Midway Atoll has served as a base for an ecotourism operation conducted under the auspices of the U.S. Fish and Wildlife Service since 1996. Midway Atoll National Wildlife Refuge accommodates visitor use such as historic preservation service projects, guided tours, diving and snorkeling trips, and fishing operations (extraction and non-extraction). In addition, Midway Atoll has been a destination for a limited number of cruise ships. For the past three years, one cruise ship per year has visited Midway (Barry Christenson [Manager, Midway Atoll National Wildlife Refuge], pers. comm.) However, visitor use in recent years has been minimal due to the lack of routine, affordable air charter service to and from Midway Atoll National Wildlife Refuge. With plans for future tourist activities around Midway Atoll, historic shipwreck sites in the vicinity may become more vulnerable to impacts from divers and snorkelers. Impacts include artifact removal and damage from improper diving techniques. Many of these impacts can be mitigated with education and outreach efforts that inform visitors of site preservation protocols (Friedlander et al. 2005).

Possible impacts from tourism at Midway include disturbance to nesting seabirds, Hawaiian monk seals, green sea turtles, spinner dolphins, fish and marine invertebrates. Visitor programs will be provided with orientation materials and will be subject to restrictions (e.g. 150 ft. approach distance for seals) intended to minimize impacts to wildlife (USFWS 2006).

Coastal Development

Coastal development in the Northwestern Hawaiian Islands has consisted of infrastructure to support a guano mining operation at Laysan Island a century ago, naval base construction at Midway and French Frigate Shoals during the first half of the 20th century, and U.S. Coast Guard LORAN station construction and operations at Kure and French Frigate Shoals for several decades following World War II. The Midway Naval Air Station supported several hundred to several thousand soldiers and dependents during pre- to post-World War II. Navigation channels for the naval bases at Midway and were

dredged during the middle of the 20th century. These types of coastal development activities alter current flow and shoreline configuration and, as a result, may significantly alter coastal erosion patterns. Operation of housing and other facilities in the past has contributed to point and nonpoint sources of pollution to the marine environment.

Since the closure of Navy and U.S. Coast Guard facilities, coastal development activities have been limited to small-scale conversion of abandoned U.S. Coast Guard buildings on Tern Island at French Frigate Shoals and Green Island at Kure to wildlife research stations (Figure 19). The only recent coastal construction has been the repair of the seawall protecting Tern Island's small runway and buildings and construction of a small boat ramp at French Frigate Shoals in 2004. Current human population levels are limited to a few workers and volunteers at wildlife stations operated at Laysan, French Frigate Shoals and Midway year round and at Kure, Lisianski, and Pearl and Hermes atolls seasonally.

Figure 19. Tern Island at French Frigate Shoals, which was enlarged during World War II to create an air strip. Today the island is part of the Hawaiian Islands National Wildlife Refuge, operated year-round as a field station by the U.S. Fish and Wildlife Service and seasonally visited by NOAA Fisheres marine mammal and sea turtle scientists and U.S. Fish and Wildlife Service seabird biologists and volunteers.

State of Monument Resources

This section provides summaries of the conditions and trends within four resource areas: water, habitat, living resources and maritime archaeological resources. For each, monument staff and selected outside experts considered a series of questions about each resource area. The set of questions derive from the National Marine Sanctuary System's mission and a system-wide monitoring framework (NMSP 2004a) developed to ensure the timely flow of data and information to those responsible for managing and protecting resources in the ocean and coastal zone, and to those that use, depend on, and study the ecosystems encompassed by the sanctuaries. Appendix A (Rating Scheme for System-Wide Monitoring Questions) clarifies the set of questions and presents statements that were used to judge the status and assign a corresponding color code on a scale from "good" to "poor." These statements are customized for each question. In addition, the following options are available for all questions: "N/A" – the question does not apply; and "undetermined" – resource status is undetermined. In addition, symbols are used to indicate trends: "▲ " – conditions appear to be improving; "—" – conditions do not appear to be changing; "▼ " – conditions appear to be declining; and "?" – trend is undetermined.

This section of the report provides answers to the set of questions. Answers are supported by specific examples of data, investigations, monitoring and observations, and the basis for judgment is provided in the text and summarized in the table for each resource area. Where published or additional information exists, the reader is provided with appropriate references and web links.

Judging an ecosystem as having "integrity" implies the relative wholeness of ecosystem structure, function, and associated complexity, along with the spatial and temporal variability inherent in these characteristics, as determined by its natural evolutionary history. Ecosystem integrity is reflected in the system's "ability to generate and maintain adaptive biotic elements through natural evolutionary process" (Angermeier and Karr 1994). The natural fluctuations of a system's native characteristics, including abiotic drivers, biotic composition, complex relationships, and functional processes are unaltered and are either likely to persist or be regained following natural disturbance.

Water

Large areas of the marine environment of the Northwestern Hawaiian Islands are considered to be nearly pristine due to their remoteness, the fact that most of the islets and shoals remain uninhabited, and the oceanographic conditions of the central Pacific Ocean. While there have been very few studies conducted on contamination, the lack of major pollution sources and the health and productivity of the coral reef ecosystems in the area strongly suggest that the marine environment is relatively unpolluted except during oil spills and other pollution discharges during ship groundings.

Although the waters surrounding the Northwestern Hawaiian Islands are minimally affected overall by anthropogenic stressors, some environmental impacts due to past human activities remain. In response to concerns by U.S. Fish and Wildlife scientists over high levels of toxic contaminants (e.g., PCBs and lead) in Northwestern Hawaiian Islands wildlife (e.g., moray eels, Hawaiian monk seals, and albatrosses), near-shore sediment sampling was conducted in 2000 (see State of "Habitat" Resources). Results of this study suggest the potential for localized water contamination, as contaminants in sediments can contribute to water quality degradation.

Satellite observations indicate a significant chlorophyll front in the area, with seasonal annual migrations (northward in the summer and southward during the winter). Should oceanographic changes

cause these nutrient-rich waters to cross the Northwestern Hawaiian Islands, productivity in the coral reef ecosystems would be expected to increase, resulting in trophic changes in the ecosystem (Friedlander et al. 2005).

The following information provides an assessment by monument staff of the status and trends pertaining to water quality and its effects on the environment:

1. Are specific or multiple stressors, including changing oceanographic and atmospheric conditions, affecting water quality and how are they changing?
The remote location of the Northwestern Hawaiian Islands has resulted in minimal anthropogenic impacts; therefore, the rating for this question is "good/fair." However, ocean acidification and temperature rise are of concern on a time scale of several decades. Acidification is projected over the next century to affect calcification by shallow and deep corals as well as other calcifying organisms, including plankton (Kleypas et al. 2006). Temperature rise has been documented in the Northwestern Hawaiian Islands and may be associated with the increasing level and frequency of coral bleaching (Jokiel and Brown 2004). Changes in the oceanographic regime, specifically the position of the sub-

tropical convergence zone, could affect productivity and other ecosystem dynamics in the region (Herman 1979). Though climate related changes may be extreme over the period of several decades, the status and trends recorded here are based on a time frame of 5 to 10 years. While impacts from acidification may not manifest in the near term, short term consequences of temperature change are more likely to be observed, possibly in the form of continued bleaching events.

2. What is the eutrophic condition of monument waters and how is it changing? The remote location of the Northwestern Hawaiian Islands has resulted in minimal anthropogenic inputs, therefore, the rating for this question is "good and not changing." However, the addition of micronutrients may occur from oxidation of discarded equipment. Climate change could also potentially affect the location of subtropical convergence and possibly result in periods of eutrophication.

3. Do monument waters pose risks to human health and how are they changing? Ciguatera has been reported in reef fishes, but humans are not typically exposed at this time because harvesting of reef fish species is not allowed (White 2007), therefore, the rating for this question is "good and not changing." It is possible that fish which is obtained through sustenance fishing (allowed on permitted vessels) or subsistence fishing (which may be permitted for traditional Native Hawaiian practices) may contain ciguatera, although fish which are likely to contain the toxin are usually avoided.

4. What are the levels of human activities that may influence water quality and how are they changing? Since the signing of the Executive Order in 2000 and the subsequent 2006 Presidential Proclamation establishing the monument there has been a reduction in human activities that could affect water quality. The number of flights to French Frigate Shoals and Midway Atoll (the only islands/atolls with landing strips in the Northwestern Hawaiian Islands), and the number of ship cruises per year decreased over the period 2005-2007. In addition, the number of people on land per day on all islands and atolls, excluding Midway, decreased over that same time period (PMNM 2008, PMNM unpublished. data). There is currently very limited access to the monument, however, there are plans to open Midway Atoll to tourism. Although previously allowed, vessels can no longer pump untreated sewage within the monument. The rating for this question is "good and improving" based on limited levels of activity and the recent prohibitions of discharges.

Water Quality Status & Trends

#	Issue	Rating	Basis for Judgment	Description of Findings
1	Stressors	▼	Published literature indicates temperature increases.	Selected conditions may preclude full development of living resource assemblages and habitats, but are not likely to cause substantial or persistent declines.
2	Eutrophic Condition	–	Lack of anthropogenic inputs.	Conditions do not appear to have the potential to negatively affect living resources or habitat quality.
3	Human Health	–	Lack of sources, causes and human exposure.	Conditions do not appear to have the potential to negatively affect human health.
4	Human Activities	▲	Limited access; regulations prohibit discharges.	Few or no activities occur that are likely to negatively affect water quality.

Status: Good Good/Fair Fair Fair/Poor Poor Undet.

Trends: Improving (▲), Not Changing (–), Declining (▼), Undetermined Trend (?), Question not applicable (N/A)

Habitat

The remoteness and limited fishing activities in the Northwestern Hawaiian Islands have resulted in minimal anthropogenic impacts of local origin on habitat resources. The reefs in the Northwestern Hawaiian Islands are among the few large-scale, intact reef ecosystems remaining in the world and offer scientists an opportunity to study how unaltered ecosystems are structured, how they function, and how they can most effectively be preserved. However, despite the limited human activity currently occurring in the Northwestern Hawaiian Islands, impacts from distant marine and past terrestrial activities have occurred.

Many of the terrestrial and nearshore habitats were physically altered by the military prior to World War II by dredging the shallow marine areas to enlarge islands at Midway, Kure and French Frigate Shoals. Subsequent military and U.S. Coast Guard operations on these islands resulted in further disturbance and contamination. Since the military and U.S. Coast Guard terminated missions on the islands, much of the contamination has been remediated and habitats are being restored. However, remaining uncharacterized and unlined landfills are contaminating seabird and sea turtle nesting areas and eroding contamination into the nearshore environment. Lead paint used on most of the structures on the islands affects albatross and other seabirds nesting near the buildings

Marine debris, mostly derelict fishing gear from distant trawl and gillnet fisheries around the Pacific Rim, is perhaps the greatest anthropogenic impact to the reefs of the Northwestern Hawaiian Islands (Figure 20). It has been estimated that at most, 900 metric tons of debris have accumulated in the Northwestern Hawaiian Islands over the past several decades. Assuming accumulation rates have been relatively constant over the past four decades, long-term average accumulation rates are approximately 47 metric tons per year (Dameron et al. 2007). Since 1996, the NOAA Fisheries Pacific Islands Fisheries Science Center has led a highly successful multi-agency effort to remove and recycle over 550 metric tons of derelict fishing gear from the Northwestern Hawaiian Islands. However, until substantial efforts are made to significantly reduce the sources of debris and until debris can be effectively removed at sea, accumulation is expected to continue indefinitely (Friedlander et al. 2005).

Past land-based human activities in the Northwestern Hawaiian Islands have also imposed potential impacts on marine habitat resources in the form of numerous toxic contaminants. Midway Atoll bears the highest levels of contamination among the Northwestern Hawaiian Islands and is primarily associated with previous military activities. Green Island at Kure Atoll, and Tern and East Islands at French Frigate Shoals were sites of former U.S. Coast Guard stations and associated PCB contamination.

Numerous studies on contamination in the monument have been conducted including remediation of the Navy's base reduction and closure at Midway, U.S. Coast Guard site assessments at Kure and French Frigate Shoals, U.S. Fish and Wildlife Service studies on fish, albatross, seals and turtles at Midway and French Frigate Shoals, and contamination in albatross at Midway. In 2000, the Northwestern Hawaiian Islands Reef Assessment and Monitoring Program conducted a survey of island near-shore sediments. Thirty-six sediment samples were analyzed for over 70 toxic contaminants. A few of the chemical concentrations were high; that is, above the 85th percentile of concentrations measured in the coastal U.S. by the NOAA National Status and Trends Program. The concentrations of organic compounds (aggregated into groups) PCB, DDT, Dieldrin, Chlordane and PAH were undetectable, very low or at least below the National Status and Trends Program median at all sites except three. One Midway site had DDT concentrations above the National Status and Trends Program median. Two other Midway sites had high levels of PCB DDT, and PAH, and one of these had a high concentration of arsenic and above-median concentrations of cadmium, lead and tin. A fourth site on Kure Atoll was the only site with high concentrations of copper and nickel (Turgeon et al. 2002, Figure 21).

The following information provides an assessment by monument staff of the status and trends pertaining to the current state of the marine habitat:

5. *What are the abundance and distribution of major habitat types and how are they changing?* The abundance and distribution of deep sea and shallow reef habitats are in good condition. However, the future of shallow habitats, which may be affected by climate change and resulting sea surface elevation, are of great concern. Much of the current beach habitats that are monk seal resting places and sea turtle nesting habitat may be greatly diminished or lost altogether with sea

Figure 20. A NOAA diver removes derelict fishing gear on Midway Atoll.

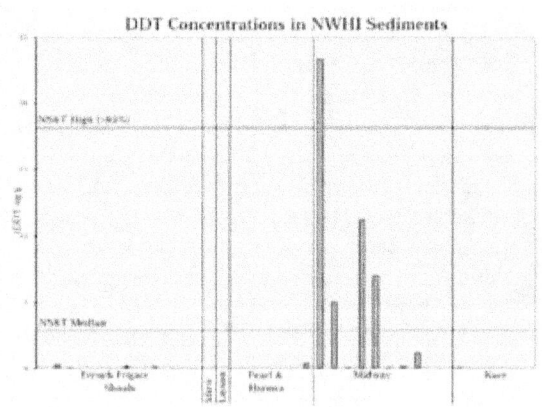

Figure 21. DDT concentrations in monument sediments.

level rise (Baker et al. 2006). Additionally, the loss of beaches at Tern Island from the creation of seawalls is of concern. The "good/fair" status rating for this question is based on the overall marine resources of the monument, but the "declining" trend reflects the need for special attention to be applied to these shallow/interface areas and beaches.

6. *What is the condition of biologically-structured habitats and how is it changing?* In general, biologically-structured habitat is in near-pristine condition; however, some localized habitats appear to be degraded due to coral bleaching and derelict fishing gear on reef structures. Therefore, the condition of biologically-structured habitats is rated as "good/fair." There have been two documented bleaching events since 2002 (Kenyon et al. 2006). Shallow habitats that have been affected by marine debris are of great concern, as derelict fishing gear is likely to have severe impacts on shallow coral habitats - there is continued accumulation of derelict fishing nets at an estimated rate of 50 tons a year (Dameron et al. 2007). In addition to the threat in general, it is specifically a threat to table coral which is documented as declining, and is a limited distribution coral. Table coral is also affected by two serious diseases, Acropora white syndrome and Acropora growth anomalies (Work et al. 2008), which are contributing to the declining populations. Unpublished data suggests that the disease is spreading from Johnston Atoll. For this reason, the trend is rated as "declining."

7. *What are the contaminant concentrations in monument habitats and how are they changing?* The remote location of the Northwestern Hawaiian Islands has resulted in minimal anthropogenic impacts, however, contamination from Navy, U.S. Coast Guard and other military operations exist at Kure, Midway and French Frigate Shoals, and there have been incidents of contaminant releases from marine debris. Therefore, the rating for this question is "good/fair and not changing." A release of the pesticide carbofuran from marine debris on the beach at Laysan caused the deaths of many animals, including several of the endangered Laysan finches (David et al. 2001). There has been an impact at Tern Island due to contaminants. Eels, crabs and other biota have been shown to have high concentrations of metals and PCBs (Miao et al. 2001). Many albatross chicks on Midway are poisoned from ingesting paint chips which contaminate the ground near buildings that were painted with lead based paint (Sileo et al. 1990). The majority of the monument is in good condition, although a few terrestrial areas and superlittoral regions have experienced varying degrees of anthropogenic impact.

8. *What are the levels of human activities that may influence habitat quality and how are they changing?* Overall levels of human activities are very low, although marine debris, climate change and remaining contamination from military and U.S. Coast Guard LORAN stations are major caveats. Therefore, because there is limited access to the site the rating for this question is "good/fair and not changing." Both marine debris and climate change are problems emanating from factors outside the monument but the effects are being felt within. Other activities include research and some bottom fishing which may affect bottom habitat through anchoring, coring or instrumentation. Permitted activities such as research comprise the majority of human activities and can be controlled. Illegal activities exist, such as unpermitted entry and access and violations by permitted bottom fishers. Such activities are difficult to quantify, but surveillance is increasing.

Habitat Status & Trends

#	Issue	Rating	Basis for Judgment	Description of Findings
5	Abundance/ Distribution	▼	Marine debris is degrading beaches and reefs. Potential loss of habitat from climate change and sea-level rise.	Selected habitat loss or alteration has taken place, precluding full development of living resource assemblages, but it is unlikely to cause substantial or persistent degradation in living resources or water quality.
6	Structure	▼	Marine debris, coral disease and perhaps bleaching frequency.	Selected habitat loss or alteration has taken place, precluding full development of living resources, but it is unlikely to cause substantial or persistent degradation in living resources or water quality.
7	Contaminants	–	Localized contamination is adversely affecting associated habitat and wildlife.	Selected contaminants may preclude full development of living resource assemblages, but are not likely to cause substantial or persistent degradation.
8	Human Activities	–	Limited visitation.	Some potentially harmful activities exist, but they do not appear to have had a negative effect on habitat quality.

Status: | Good | Good/Fair | Fair | Fair/Poor | Poor | Undet. |

Trends: Improving (▲), Not Changing (–), Declining (▼), Undetermined Trend (?), Question not applicable (N/A)

Living Resources

Coral reefs in the Northwestern Hawaiian Islands are among the few remaining large-scale, intact, predator-dominated reef ecosystems left in the world. Areas with the highest apex predator biomass include Pearl and Hermes Atoll, followed by Lisianski and Laysan Islands. Apex predator biomass of the Northwestern Hawaiian Islands is about 55 percent of the total fish biomass, whereas this trophic level accounts for less than three percent of the fish biomass in the main Hawaiian Islands (Figure 22). Apex predator biomass on fore-reef habitats in the Northwestern Hawaiian Islands is 1.3 metric tons per hectare compared to less than 0.05 metric tons per hectare in the main Hawaiian Islands. Overall, reef fish standing stock in the monument is more than 260 percent greater than the main Hawaiian Islands across similar habitats (Friedlander et al. 2005).

Coral reef ecosystems consist of much more than the reef-building corals for which they are named. Coral reefs also include sand and unconsolidated sediments, colonized hard-bottom, non-reef-building corals, crustose coralline algae and macroalgae. Corals are the keystone organisms of this ecosystem, comprising approximately 50 percent of the biomass and providing habitat structure, refuge and food to a diverse group of microscopic organisms and crustaceans, mollusks, fish and other species of the tropical reef environment (Garrison 1999).

Endangered Species

The Northwestern Hawaiian Islands host more than 7,000 species including marine mammals, fishes, sea turtles, birds, invertebrates and marine algae. Twenty-three species of plants and animals known to occur in the Northwestern Hawaiian Islands are listed under the Endangered Species Act. Of particular concern are the Hawaiian monk seal and green sea turtle. Recently the Northwestern Hawaiian Islands have been identified as providing extensive wintering habitat for humpback whales, *Megaptera novaeangliae* (Johnston et al. 2007).

Hawaiian Monk Seals – Hawaiian monk seals are distributed throughout Hawaii predominantly in six Northwestern Hawaiian Islands subpopulations at French Frigate Shoals, Laysan and Lisianski Islands, Pearl and Hermes Reef, and Midway and Kure Atoll. The current population size of the Hawaiian monk seal is estimated between 1,200 and 1,300 individuals and depends almost entirely on the islands of the Northwestern Hawaiian Islands for breeding and the surrounding reefs for sustenance. Reproductive success has declined, with a total of mean non-pup beach counts at the main reproductive Northwestern Hawaiian Islands subpopulations in 2003 approximately 60 percent lower than in 1958 (Figure 23).

Trends in abundance vary considerably among the six main subpopulations. For example, the decline since the mid-1980s was largely due to a severe decline at French Frigate Shoals, where non-pup beach counts decreased by 70 percent from 1989-2003. Populations at Laysan and Lisianski Islands have remained relatively stable since approximately 1990, though the former has tended to increase slightly while the latter has decreased slowly.

Until recently, populations at Kure, Midway, and Pearl and Hermes reef exhibited substantial growth. The subpopulation at Kure Atoll grew at an average rate of five percent per year from 1983 to 2000, due largely to decreased human disturbance and introduced females. Since 2000, counts at Kure have declined coinciding with very low survival of the 2000-2002 cohorts from weaning to age 1 year (15 percent to 22 percent). The subpopulation at Pearl and Hermes Reef increased after the mid-1970s, however, growth of this subpopulation has slowed recently and early survival has declined. Recovery of the small subpopulation at Midway Atoll appears to have slowed or stopped, also

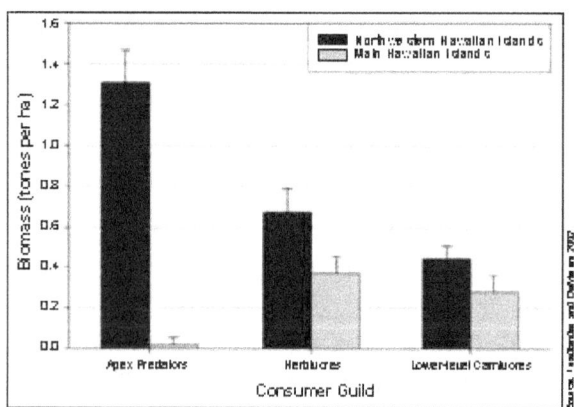

Figure 22. Comparison of the biomass in major trophic guilds between the main Hawaiian Islands and the Northwestern Hawaiian Islands.

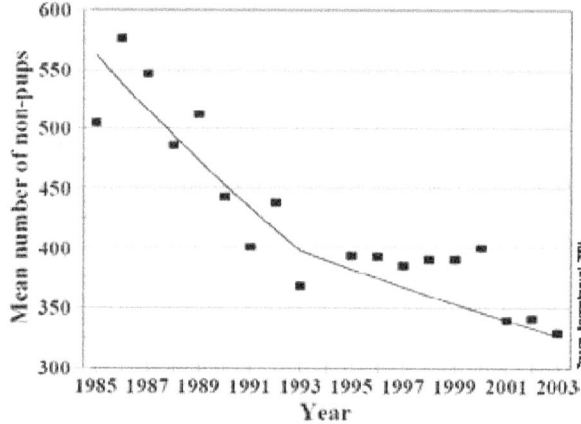

Figure 23. Mean beach counts of Hawaiian monk seals at the six main Northwestern Hawaiian Islands subpopulations, 1985-2003.

accompanied by relatively poor juvenile survival. These declines may be related to reduced food sources or increasing competition for prey items with apex predators, fewer pupping sites and increased predation of pups by sharks. Implementation of the National Marine Fisheries Service *2006 Recovery Plan for the Hawaiian Monk Seal* will hopefully result in an upward trend in seals before the population of reproductive female seals decline to precipitous levels (NMFS 2005, NMFS 2006).

Green Sea Turtles – The green sea turtle was listed as threatened in 1978. Although the population has increased significantly since the 1970s, the total number of nesting females is still well below the historical levels of the late 1800s (Figure 24). However, the Hawaiian green sea turtle stock is clearly recovering after more than 25 years of protecting their nesting and foraging habitats in the Hawaiian Archipelago (Balazs and Chaloupka 2003). Over 90 percent of all sub-adult and adult green turtles found throughout Hawaii come from the Northwestern Hawaiian Islands. The primary nesting site for green turtles is French Frigate Shoals, which accounts for 400 nesting sites or 90 percent of all nesting within the Hawaiian Archipelago. Nesting also occurs at Pearl and Hermes Atoll and Lisianski Island. However, massive beach and island erosion witnessed at the principal nesting island in 2006 (Eastern Island, French Frigate Shoals) may reduce the number of suitable nesting sites for turtles or reduce the survivorship of hatchlings (NMSP 2005).

Nesting Seabirds – The importance of seabirds in the Northwestern Hawaiian Islands was recognized in 1909 with the establishment of the Hawaiian Islands National Wildlife Refuge. Early protection and active management in the Northwestern Hawaiian Islands resulted in large and diverse seabird populations. The conservation status of Hawaiian seabirds was more recently assessed as part of the North American Waterbird Conservation Plan (Kushlan et al. 2002). Eight

Figure 25. The Christmas Shearwater can grow to have a wing span of up to nearly 32 inches. Adults return to colonies in the Northwestern Hawaiian Islands in March and depart in early fall.

of the 22 species that breed in the Northwestern Hawaiian Islands were classified as highly imperiled or of high conservation concern at the broad scale of the plan (eastern North Pacific, western North Atlantic and Caribbean). At the regional scale (Pacific Islands) five of the breeding species were included in these highest concern categories: Laysan and Black-footed Albatrosses, Christmas Shearwater (Figure 25), Tristram's Storm-petrel and Blue Noddy.

The greatest threats to seabirds in the Northwestern Hawaiian Islands have been introduced mammals (e.g., rabbits, rats and mice) and other invasive species, fishery interactions, contaminants, oil pollution, marine debris and climate change. Over the past 20 years, active management in the National Wildlife Refuges and State Seabird Sanctuary has included eradication of black rats at Midway Atoll and Polynesian rats at Kure Atoll; eradication or control of invasive plants; cleanup of contaminants and hazards at former military sites; and coordination with NOAA Fisheries, Regional Fishery Management Councils, industry and conservation organizations to reduce fishing impacts.

Introduced Species

Eleven species of shallow-water snapper and grouper were purposefully introduced to the main islands of the Hawaiian Archipelago in the late 1950s and early 1960s. Two snappers, the bluestripe snapper (Figure 26) and the blacktail snapper, and one grouper, the peacock grouper, are well-established and have documented pat-

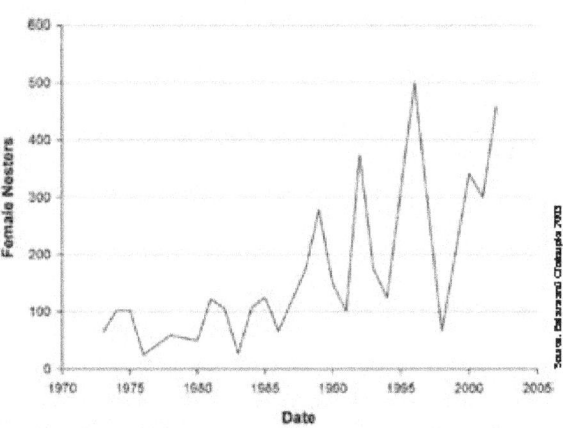

Figure 24. Nester abundance shown as the number of female green sea turtles nesting each year at East Island (French Frigate Shoals) from 1973 to 2002.

Figure 26. Bluestripe snappers (Lutjanus kasmira, or "ta'ape") were introduced to the main Hawaiian Islands in the late 1950s for commercial fishing and have since spread to Midway at the opposite end of the Hawaiian archipelago.

terns of colonization along the island chain (Randall 1987). Blues-tripe snappers have been by far the most successful fish introduction to the Hawaiian coral reef ecosystem. From some 3,200 individuals introduced on the island of Oahu in the 1950s, the population has expanded its range by 1,491 miles and has been reported as far north as Midway in the Northwestern Hawaiian Islands. These records suggest a dispersal rate of about 20 to 80 miles per year. The other two species have only been recorded as far north as French Frigate Shoals and are present in much lower numbers than bluestripe snappers (Friedlander et al. 2005).

The following information provides an assessment by monument staff of the status and trends pertaining to the current state of the monument's living resources:

9. *What is the status of biodiversity and how is it changing?* The research community is still in an exploratory phase with its understanding of biodiversity. Therefore, the rating of "good and not changing" for this question is based on limited existing information. There are known terrestrial extinctions; however, this document is limited to the marine environment and therefore these extinctions are not considered in the assessment.

Ongoing characterization and exploration is yielding new information on biodiversity at a rapid rate. A recent Census of Marine Life Cruise to French Frigate Shoals uncovered 30 to 50 invertebrate species new to science, 58 new ascidian records, 33 new records of decapod crustaceans, and 27 new opisto-branch mollusks of record (R. Brainard, NOAA NMFS, pers. comm.). Hawaii Undersea Research Lab (HURL) submersible cruises in 2007 discovered several new genera of octocorals, as well as sponges that are likely new to science (C. Kelley, HURL, pers. comm.). Even in the relatively well-explored shallow coral reef areas, ongoing characterizations of crustose coralline algal communities are finding species or morphologies that are distinct from those of the Main Hawaiian Islands (I. Abbott, University of Hawai'i, pers. comm.).

10. *What is the status of environmentally sustainable fishing and how is it changing?* The only substantial fishery in the Northwestern Hawaiian Islands is for bottomfish. Population analysis by NOAA Fisheries indicates these fisheries are operating at fishing levels below that required to harvest Maximum Sustainable Yield (WPRFMC 1986). Spawning potential ratio indicates that presently the overall the status of the fishery is good. Therefore, this question is rated "good." The trend for this question is rated as "improving" because regulations will phase out bottomfishing in five years from the date of proclamation (due to be enforced in 2011).

11. *What is the status of non-indigenous species and how is it changing?* The status rating for this question is "good/fair" because few non-indigenous species have been documented. However, there is uncertainty of potential impacts from these species; therefore, the trend is "undetermined." Eleven species are documented, but not all are established. Only two invasive species are found throughout the monument (Godwin et al. 2005); the blueline snapper (ta'ape) and the hydroid Pennaria. Distribution of the latter is limited within the monument; the majority of established individuals are in Midway harbor. The primary source of invasive species is the main islands, and management processes are in place. Marine debris is a potential vector but is not within management control.

12. *What is the status of key species and how is it changing?* Key species in the monument include those functioning as apex predators, such as sharks and jacks, habitat forming corals, and protected species such as turtles, monk seals and seabirds. Status of these groups of species varies considerably. Apex predators are in near pristine condition in the monument (Friedlander and DeMartini 2002), and coral (Friedlander et al. 2005) and turtle (Balazs and Chaloupka 2003) populations appear to be holding steady. Monk seals, on the other hand, have suffered a 60 percent population decline since the 1950s (Antonelis 2004) and are currently at critically low levels. The reasons for the earlier declines are generally agreed on as being the result of prior human disturbance of habitats (during island occupation and exploitation expeditions; Kenyon 1972) and hunting (Clapp and Woodward 1972).

Continued declines of monk seals after the 1950s are debated and most likely related to a combination of factors, including shark predation (Bertilsson-Friedman 2002), which affects both adult and juvenile survival (Craig and Ragan 1999), disrupted sex ratios that have enhanced levels of male aggression, food limitation (Gilmartin 1993, Craig and Ragen 1999) caused by decadal shifts in patterns of productivity (Polovina et al 1994) that affect fish abundances, inbreeding within the small remaining population, marine debris entanglement (Henderson 2001), and episodic events like ciguatera poisoning (Gilmartin et al 1980). The potential for monk seal recovery is uncertain, as some factors would indicate enormous challenges (e.g., the paucity of reproductively active females) while others suggest cause for optimism (the increasing number in the Main Hawaiian Islands; NMFS 2007).

The overall rating of "fair" for this question was considered to be reasonable, given the decline of the monk seal populations in the monument and the relatively high and stable populations of corals and predatory fish at the site. The "undetermined" trend is based on the uncertainty regarding monk seal recovery.

13. *What is the condition or health of key species and how is it changing?*

Surveys in some locations indicate that many yearling, juvenile, and adult female monk seals are in poor health. Emaciated animals and females with low reproductive performance may be associated with food limitation (Gilmartin 1993). Animals have also been found with severe injuries that compromise their condition. At French Frigate Shoals, this led investigators to suggest that shark predation increased after 1987 (Bertilsson-Friedman 2002). The health of a few species of seabirds has also declined, caused by the ingestion of lead based paint and plastics and possibly the bioaccumulation of marine toxins. On the other hand, with the exception of occasional encounters of diseased individuals, predatory and reef fishes, marine invertebrates, and most corals appear stable and in good condition. The rating of "fair" for this question primarily considers the compromised condition of monk seal and seabirds. The "undetermined" trend is based on the uncertainty regarding monk seal condition and health.

14. *What are the levels of human activities that may influence living resource quality and how are they changing?*

Overall levels of human activities are very low, although marine debris and climate change are major factors that threaten Northwestern Hawaiian Islands habitats and ultimately the health of key species (Baker et al. 2006). Therefore, the rating for this question is "good/fair and not changing." Both marine debris and climate change are affected by human activities occurring far outside the monument but the effects are being felt within. Other activities include research and some bottom fishers. Permitted activities such as research comprise the majority of human activities and can be controlled, and fishing will be phased out by 2011. Illegal activities exist and are difficult to quantify, but surveillance is increasing.

Living Resources Status & Trends

#	Issue	Rating	Basis for Judgment	Description of Findings
9	Biodiversity	–	Assessment/ monitoring activities to date.	Biodiversity appears to reflect pristine or near-pristine conditions and promotes ecosystem integrity (full community development and function).
10	Extracted Species	▲	Limited activity; existing fishery to be phased out by June 2011.	Extraction does not appear to affect ecosystem integrity (full community development and function).
11	Non-Indigenous Species	?	Few species with isolated distributions; uncertainty of potential impact.	Non-indigenous species exist, precluding full community development and function, but are unlikely to cause substantial or persistent degradation of ecosystem integrity.
12	Key Species Status	?	Monk seal decline; corals and predatory fish populations high and stable.	The reduced abundance of selected keystone species may inhibit full community development and function and may cause measurable but not severe degradation of ecosystem integrity; or selected key species are at reduced levels, but recovery is possible.
13	Key Species Condition	?	Monk seal starvation and body condition; debris ingestion by seabirds; predatory fish and most corals in good condition and stable.	The diminished condition of selected key resources may cause a measurable but not severe reduction in ecological function, but recovery is possible.
14	Human Activities	–	Limited visitation.	Some potentially harmful activities exist, but they do not appear to have had a negative effect on living resource quality.

Status: | Good | Good/Fair | Fair | Fair/Poor | Poor | Undet. |

Trends: Improving (▲), Not Changing (–), Declining (▼), Undetermined Trend (?), Question not applicable (N/A)

Maritime Archaeological Resources

Due to the strategic location of the Northwestern Hawaiian Islands for commerce and military activities, the area features significant maritime heritage resources. Beginning in 2002, archaeologists with NOAA's Maritime Heritage Program have been conducting the systematic survey of important wreck sites in the Northwestern Hawaiian Islands and sharing their findings with the public through a comprehensive education and outreach program. Of the current 127 potential resource sites, 20 preliminary site assessments have been conducted, and nine site inventory surveys have been completed. Resources include British and American 19th-century whaling shipwrecks, the U.S. Navy side wheel steamer USS Saginaw, the World War II submarine rescue vessel USS Macaw, and the American bark Carrollton. Maritime archaeological survey in the Northwestern Hawaiian Islands emphasizes a non-invasive approach, in situ management being the preferred alternative. This approach is most compatible with the goal of minimizing or eliminating negative impacts on the ecosystem. The comprehensive survey to locate and assess all existing maritime heritage sites, as directed by the National Historic Preservation Act, has not been completed.

The following information provides an assessment by maritime heritage staff from the Pacific Islands regional office of the status and trends pertaining to the current state of the monument's maritime archaeological resources. It is important to remember that, while the Northwestern Hawaiian Islands possess unique examples of heritage resources, the systematic survey of these sites has only recently begun. These surveys are currently conducted by a small team of maritime archaeologists, accompanying biologists and oceanographers on "piggy-back" missions of opportunity. Site archaeological inventory is time-intensive, and completion of a survey often requires work over multiple field seasons. This means that estimates of resource status at this point are often based on partial data.

15. What is the integrity of known maritime archaeological resources and how is it changing? Resource integrity is carefully defined by the National Register for Historic Places as a crucial measure for heritage sites. Measures of integrity include location, design, setting, materials, workmanship, feeling and association. Integrity does not simply mean the "intactness" of a shipwreck or structure, for the same types of measures apply to scattered sites and artifacts as well, provided the site retains historical, scientific or educational information. The integrity of known maritime archaeological resources in the monument is rated "fair" because deterioration has resulted from natural biological, chemical, and physical processes. Shallow water heritage resources in the Northwestern Hawaiian Islands have often been broken apart by the high-energy environment but retain a measure of integrity as pristine archaeological sites. The "declining" trend is due to the slow and inevitable processes of deterioration over time.

16. Do known maritime archaeological resources pose an environmental hazard and how is this threat changing? From the handful of archaeological resources which have been surveyed to date, there are no known hazardous cargoes on archaeological sites currently threatening the environment. Therefore, the rating for this question is "good and not changing." Historical and archaeological sites are considered to be at least 50 years in age, lowering the immediate threat of damage from mechanical break-up. Nineteenth -century shipwreck sites exhibit even less potential impact, coming closer to a state of equilibrium with their immediate environment. World War II-era vessels that may have hazardous cargoes or materials have been lost in the Northwestern Hawaiian Islands, but these have not yet been surveyed or located. Modern wrecks that are not archaeologi-

cal resources may pose a threat from deterioration, and surveys of these impact sites should be conducted in the future.

17. What are the levels of human activities that may influence maritime archaeological resource quality and how are they changing? While there do exist anecdotal reports of maritime archaeological resources having been removed illegally from the Northwestern Hawaiian Islands in the past, these instances have not been fully documented or confirmed. In general, the remoteness of the Northwestern Hawaiian Islands protects its archaeological sites compared with other, more accessible locations. Therefore, the rating for this question is "good and improving." Management efforts currently include education and outreach focusing on the nature of archaeological resources and heritage preservation, and this is one of the best long-term strategies for minimizing potential human impacts. Damage and/or removal of archaeological resources remain a concern, and planned future activities (such as tourism at specific locations) indicate the necessity of outreach, monitoring and enforcement. Archaeological resources are also subject to inadvertent damage in a similar manner to the natural ecosystem from anchors, marine debris, groundings, etc.

Maritime Archaeological Resources Status & Trends

#	Issue	Rating	Basis for Judgment	Description of Findings
15	Integrity	▼	Natural deterioration (physical, biological and chemical).	The diminished condition of selected archaeological resources has reduced, to some extent, their historical, scientific or educational value and may affect the eligibility of some sites for listing in the National Register of Historic Places.
16	Threat to Environment	—	No known resources with hazardous cargos.	Known maritime archaeological resources pose few or no environmental threats.
17	Human Activities	▲	Few instances of resource removal or damage.	Few or no activities occur that are likely to negatively affect maritime archaeological resource integrity.

Status: **Good** **Good/Fair** Fair Fair/Poor Poor Undet.

Trends: Improving (▲), Not Changing (—), Declining (▼), Undetermined Trend (**?**), Question not applicable (**N/A**)

Response to Pressures

This section provides a summary of existing and proposed responses to pressures on marine resources of the Northwestern Hawaiian Islands. Existing monument responses and management actions are enacted to implement the final Papahānaumokuākea Marine National Monument regulations issued by NOAA and U.S. Fish and Wildlife Service on August 29, 2006, that codify the prohibitions and management measures set forth in Presidential Proclamation 8031. The Monument Co-Trustees developed a joint management plan, containing 22 action plans that address six priority management needs, which was released in December 2008.

Jurisdictional Authorities of the Monument

The three principal entities (collectively known as the Co-Trustees) with responsibility for managing lands and waters of the monument are the Secretary of Commerce through NOAA, the Secretary of the Interior through the U.S. Fish and Wildlife Service and the State of Hawaii through the Governor.

The State of Hawaii, Department of Land and Natural Resources has stewardship responsibility for managing, administering and exercising control over coastal and submerged lands, ocean waters and marine resources under state jurisdiction out to three miles offshore of each of the Northwestern Hawaiian Islands, except Midway which was excluded by the Hawaii Statehood Act of 1959. The state currently manages the emergent lands and reefs at Kure Atoll as a State Wildlife Sanctuary. U.S. Fish and Wildlife Service has primary responsibility for management of the areas of the monument that overlay the Midway Atoll National Wildlife Refuge and the Battle of Midway National Memorial, as well as the terrestrial areas of the Hawaiian Islands National Wildlife Refuge. NOAA has primary management responsibility of marine areas of the monument. A Memorandum of Agreement signed by all three trustees on December 8, 2006, created a jurisdictional regime where all parties share in the management, access and permissions to enter the monument, and which will normally require a consensus among all trustees for important decisions affecting the monument. The co-trustees have established

Entering the Monument

Entering the monument is prohibited without prior notification (uninterrupted passage only), except where necessary to respond to emergencies threatening life, property, or the environment, or activities necessary for law enforcement purposes or armed forces actions.

a goal to provide a seamless and unified management in the spirit of cooperative conservation (71 FR 51134).

In coordination with the Secretary of Commerce, the Western Pacific Regional Fishery Management Council is tasked with stewardship over fishery resources in the Exclusive Economic Zone (generally 3 to 200 miles offshore) surrounding the Northwestern Hawaiian Islands, under the Magnuson Fishery Conservation and Management Act of 1976. The council has developed fishery management plans for bottomfish, crustaceans, pelagic fisheries and precious corals in the Northwestern Hawaiian Islands. Due to the regulations set forth in Proclamation 8031, which established the monument, some of these fisheries are now closed. In 1996, the Sustainable Fisheries Act made NOAA Fisheries in affiliation with the council also responsible for protecting essential fish habitat (NMSP 2005).

Figure 27. The NOAA research vessel Hi'ialakai is homeported in Hawaii to support coral reef ecosystem mapping and habitat activities in the greater Pacific under the NOAA Ocean Service.

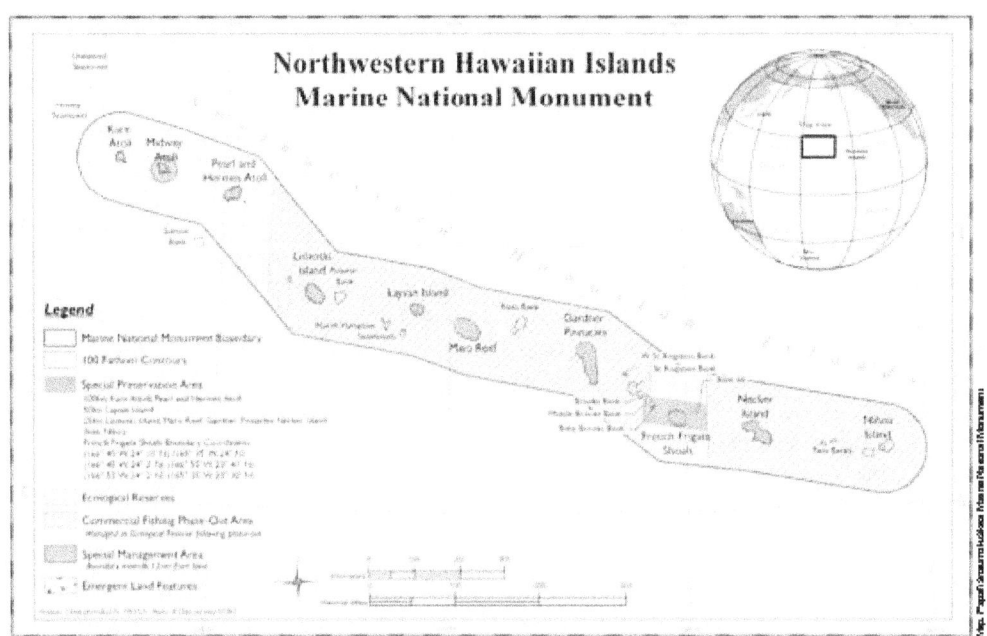

Figure 28. Map of monument boundaries, special preservation and management areas, ecological reserves, and commercial fishing phase-out areas.

Special Preservation Areas and Ecological Reserves

Special Preservation Areas are discrete, biologically important areas of the monument (Figure 28). Uses within special preservation areas are subject to conditions, restrictions and prohibitions, including but not limited to access restrictions. Special preservation areas are used to avoid concentrations of uses that could result in declines in species populations or habitats, to reduce conflicts between uses, to protect areas that are critical for sustaining important marine species or habitats, or to provide opportunities for scientific research.

Ecological Reserves are areas of the monument consisting of contiguous, diverse habitats that provide natural spawning, nursery and permanent residence areas for the replenishment and genetic protection of marine life, and also to protect and preserve natural assemblages of habitats and species within areas representing a broad diversity of resources and habitats found within the monument.

The Special Preservation Areas cover a total area of 6,802 square miles, including the 924-square mile Midway Atoll Special Management Area. The Ecological Reserves cover a total of 37,762 square miles.

NOAA and U.S. Fish and Wildlife Service monument regulations for special preservation areas and special management areas state that except due to emergencies and law enforcement activities, the following activities are prohibited without a valid permit:

■ Discharging or depositing any material or other matter into special preservation areas or the Midway Atoll Special Management Area except vessel engine cooling water, weather deck runoff and vessel engine exhaust; and

■ Swimming, snorkeling, or closed or open circuit SCUBA diving within any special preservation area or Midway Atoll Special Management Area.

Marine Pollution

Impacts of marine debris upon the ecological health of the Northwestern Hawaiian Islands have not been fully documented due to the large size and remoteness of the region, as well as the historical and ongoing nature of the problem. Mortality as the result of entanglement in derelict fishing gear, primarily nets, has been documented for several mobile marine species in the Northwestern Hawaiian Islands with impact upon the Hawaiian monk seal being of greatest concern due to its highly endangered status. In November 2006, NOAA Fisheries developed the Recovery Plan for the Hawaiian Monk Seal with the goal of assuring the long-term viability of the Hawaiian monk seal in the wild, allowing initially for reclassification to threatened status and, ultimately, removal from the List of Endangered and Threatened Wildlife (NMFS 2006).

On July 13, 2007, the monument was designated "in principle" as a Particularly Sensitive Sea Area by the International Maritime Organization, a Specialized Agency of the United Nations. Particularly Sensitive Sea Area designation will augment domestic protective measures by alerting international mariners to exercise extreme caution when navigating through the area. Additionally, as part of the designation process, in July 2007 the International Maritime Organization's Sub-Committee on Safety of Navigation approved U.S. proposals for the associated protective measures of: (1) the expansion and amendment of the six existing areas to be avoided in the area, which would enlarge the class of vessels to which they apply and augment the geographic scope of these areas as well as add new areas to be avoided around Kure and Midway atolls; and (2) the establishment of a ship reporting system for vessels transiting the monument, which is mandatory for US ships and foreign vessels (> 300 gross tons) entering or departing a U.S. port, and which is recommended for all other ships.

Ultimately, the monument's desired outcome is the elimination of marine debris and derelict fishing gear from the Northwestern Hawaiian Islands. Complete elimination of marine debris in the near future is virtually impossible due to the financial cost, the size of the area and continual influx of new debris. However, removal of existing debris, detection and prevention of incoming debris, and education to prevent generation of more debris are the achievable strategies to reduce its overall impact. The following management strategies have been identified to reduce the impact of marine debris:

■ Contributing to the Northwestern Hawaiian Islands marine debris removal effort and developing and implementing a five-year marine debris removal and prevention plan for the monument.

■ Supporting NOAA Fisheries marine debris studies; working with the U.S. State Department to gain international cooperation and involvement for marine debris issues; working with the fishery management councils to address marine debris prevention with U.S. fishing fleets; and working with partners to continue to develop and implement an outreach strategy for marine debris.

Existing NOAA and U.S. Fish and Wildlife Service monument regulations that address marine pollution within monument waters are:

■ Exploring for, developing or producing oil, gas or minerals is prohibited within the monument.

■ Except due to emergencies and law enforcement activities, discharging or depositing any material or other matter into the monument, or discharging or depositing any material or other matter outside the monument that subsequently enters the monument

and injures any resources of the monument, except fish parts (i.e., chumming material or bait) used in and during authorized fishing operations, or discharges incidental to vessel use such as deck wash, approved marine sanitation device effluent, cooling water and engine exhaust is prohibited (71 FR 51134).

Diseases, Climate Change and Coral Bleaching

With coral reefs around the world in decline, the Northwestern Hawaiian Islands present a unique opportunity to characterize an intact coral reef ecosystem and to begin to understand the degree of natural variability in an ecosystem relatively free of local anthropogenic influences. Studying these remote ecosystems may also make an important contribution toward understanding the impacts of global climate change on coral reefs.

The monument's goal is to increase understanding of the distributions and functional linkages of marine organisms and their habitats in space and time to improve ecosystem-based management decisions. The following strategies have been identified to support continued characterization and monitoring of Northwestern Hawaiian Islands marine ecosystems:

■ Assess and prioritize research and monitoring activities by: developing and implementing a prioritized research and monitoring plan for the monument and update annually; and coordinating meetings for research updates with researchers.

■ Conduct research that supports ecosystem-based management by: continuing to characterize types and spatial distributions of shallow-water marine habitats; working with partners to map and characterize deep-water habitats; conducting a biogeographic assessment of Northwestern Hawaiian Islands living marine resources; implementing additional research priorities identified in the Monument Research and Monitoring Plan; and facilitating and supporting the development of ecosystem models.

■ Conduct monitoring to understand ecosystem change over time by: assessing monitoring program protocols; formalizing a collaborative regional monitoring program for the Northwestern Hawaiian Islands; continuing to monitor at established sites in shallow-water coral reef; establishing a monitoring program for deep-water ecosystems; and collecting, analyzing and inputting research, monitoring and bathymetric data into appropriate databases to inform management decisions.

■ Communicate results of research and monitoring by: coordinating an annual meeting to present current research being conducted in the Northwestern Hawaiian Islands; prioritizing research, monitoring and modeling projects for education and outreach; including an educational component in all research expeditions; and using materials gathered and created during research expeditions to develop or enhance education and output products.

Alien Species

Because it is difficult, if not impossible, to determine whether an alien species will become invasive in a given environment, efforts must be made to prevent all alien species from entering Northwestern Hawaiian Islands ecosystems. Three strategies have been identified for achieving the desired outcomes of preventing alien species introductions and monitoring and controlling existing alien species in the monument:

■ Prevent, monitor and control alien species introductions by: developing an interagency Northwestern Hawaiian Islands alien species plan to address prevention, control and response and develop best management practices; conducting hull inspections and cleaning for NOAA research vessels to prevent the introduction of marine alien species to the Northwestern Hawaiian Islands; developing a hull inspection and cleaning program for vessels operating under permit in special preservation areas to prevent the introduction of marine alien species to the Northwestern Hawaiian Islands; identifying, characterizing and monitoring populations of alien species; conducting research on alien species detection and control; and working with partners in responding to alien species introductions in the Northwestern Hawaiian Islands.

■ Engage monument users and the public in preventing the introduction and spread of alien species by: integrating alien species information into an overall outreach program for monument permittees and integrating alien species information into general monument outreach materials.

■ Participate in statewide and Pacific regional alien species efforts by participating in statewide and international initiatives on alien species.

Existing NOAA and U.S. Fish and Wildlife Service monument regulations that address marine alien species within monument waters are (71 FR 51134):

■ Introducing or otherwise releasing an introduced species from within or into the monument is prohibited.

■ Except due to emergencies and law enforcement activities, discharging or depositing any material or other matter into the monument is prohibited (see Marine Pollution for further details).

■ Hull cleaning and inspections required for all vessels permitted to enter the monument

Fishing

Existing NOAA, U.S. Fish and Wildlife Service, and State of Hawaii regulations that address fishing activities within monument waters are:

■ Using or attempting to use poisons, electrical charges or explosives in the collection or harvest of a monument resource is prohibited.

a. Commercial fishing regulations within the monument are as follows:

■ Lobster fishing. The Presidential Proclamation has permanently closed the commercial lobster fishery within the monument.

■ Fishing and bottomfish and pelagic species.

° Commercial fishing for bottomfish and associated pelagic species may continue within the monument subject to general requirements (below), until June 15, 2011, provided that: (i) the fishing is conducted in accordance with a valid commercial bottomfish permit issued by NOAA; and (ii) such permit was in effect on June 15, 2006, and is subsequently renewed pursuant to NOAA regulations.
° Total landings for each fishing year may not exceed the following amounts: (i) 350,000 pounds for bottomfish species; and (ii) 180,000 pounds for pelagic species.
° Commercial fishing for bottomfish and associated pelagic species is prohibited in the monument after June 15, 2011.

■ General requirements. Any commercial fishing within the monument shall be conducted in accordance with the following restrictions and conditions:
° A valid permit or facsimile of a valid permit shall be on board the fishing vessel and available for inspection by an authorized officer;
° No attempt is made to falsify or fail to make, keep, maintain or submit any logbook or logbook form or other required record or report;
° Only gear specifically authorized by the relevant permit issued under the Magnuson-Stevens Fishery Conservation and Management Act is allowed to be in the possession of a person conducting commercial fishing under this section;
° Any person conducting commercial fishing notifies the Secretaries by telephone, facsimile or electronic mail at least 72 hours before entering the monument and within 12 hours after leaving the monument in accordance with federal regulations;
° All fishing vessels must carry an activated and functioning ves-

sel monitoring system unit on board at all times whenever the vessel is in the monument;

° All fishing vessels must carry an observer when requested to do so by the Secretaries;

° The activity does not take place within any ecological reserve, any special preservation area or within either national wildlife refuge.

b. Except where necessary to respond to emergencies threatening life, property or the environment, or activities necessary for law enforcement purposes or armed forces actions, the following activities are prohibited throughout the monument (71 FR 51134):

■ Removing, moving, taking, harvesting, possessing, injuring, disturbing or damaging, or attempting to remove, move, take, harvest, possess, injure, disturb or damage any living or nonliving monument resource;

■ Possessing fishing gear except when stowed and not available for immediate use during passage without interruption through the monument;

■ Attracting any living monument resource

Vessel Hazards and Groundings

Vessel activities can introduce hazards to the marine environment. Some are biological in nature (e.g., the threat of alien species introductions and interactions with protected marine species). Other environmental threats from vessels include waste, effluent, and bilge and ballast water discharge, light and noise pollution, and anchor damage. Two strategies have been identified for achieving the desired outcome of preventing and reducing impacts of vessels operating in and transiting through Northwestern Hawaiian Islands:

■ Address known vessel hazards and impacts by: developing protocols and practices for safe vessel operations with jurisdictional partners; informing monument users about hazards, regulations, permit requirements and compliance regarding vessel operations; investigating domestic and international shipping designations; and working with NOAA and the U.S. Coast Guard to update nautical charts and Notice to Mariners.

■ Conduct research on vessel hazards and impacts by conducting a vessel threat assessment and conducting studies on vessel hazards and impacts.

NOAA and U.S. Fish and Wildlife Service monument regulations stipulate that except due to emergencies and law enforcement activities,

deserting a vessel aground, at anchor, or adrift is prohibited within the monument (71 FR 51134).

Tourism and Recreation

Ocean-based ecotourism and recreation in their various forms can provide significant educational opportunities, build constituencies and provide assistance to natural resource managers. However, they can also lead to wildlife disturbance, habitat degradation and pollution. It is a goal of the monument to prevent, avoid or minimize negative human impacts associated with ocean-based ecotourism and recreation by allowing access only for those activities that do not threaten the natural character or biological integrity of the Northwestern Hawaiian Islands ecosystem or Native Hawaiian cultural or maritime heritage resources. The Midway Atoll Visitor Services Action Plan, a section of the recently completed Monument Management Plan, guides visitor activities. The plan documents approved recreational activities at Midway Atoll and ensures that they are compatible with the mission and objectives of the refuge, the national memorial and the monument. A special ocean use permit could be issued for such activities meeting the specific requirements specified in the monument regulations. The monument co-trustees will continue to assess and manage recreation and ocean-based ecotourism activities by: working with the Interagency Coordinating Committee to identify locations that may be suitable for ocean-based ecotourism; tracking and assessing recreational activities; and developing outreach materials specific to recreational uses and integrating them into a permitting outreach program.

Existing NOAA and U.S. Fish and Wildlife Service monument regulations that address tourism and recreation within monument waters are:

■ Anchoring on or having a vessel anchored on any living or dead coral with an anchor, anchor chain or anchor rope is prohibited within the monument.

■ Except due to emergencies and law enforcement activities, removing, moving, taking, harvesting, possessing, injuring, disturbing, damaging, or attempting to remove, move, take, harvest, possess, injure, disturb, or damage any living or nonliving resource; drilling into, dredging or otherwise altering the submerged lands other than by anchoring a vessel; constructing, placing or abandoning any structure, material, or other matter on the submerged lands; touching coral, living or dead; possessing fishing gear except when stowed and not available for immediate use during passage without interruption through the monument; and attracting any living resource is prohibited within the monument (71 FR 51134).

Protected Species

There are three federal acts, as well as multiple state statutes, that protect specific species in the Northwestern Hawaiian Islands. The federal acts are the Endangered Species Act, the Marine Mammal Protection Act and the Migratory Bird Treaty Act. The Endangered Species Act of 1973 provides for the conservation of species at risk of extinction throughout all or a significant portion of their range and the conservation of the ecosystems on which they depend. The Marine Mammal Protection Act of 1972 established a moratorium, with certain exceptions, on the taking of marine mammals in U.S. waters and by U.S. citizens on the high seas, and on the importing of marine mammals and marine mammal products into the United States. The Migratory Bird Treaty Act of 1918 implements various treaties and conventions between the United States and Canada, Japan, Mexico and the former Soviet Union for the protection of migratory birds.

Although endangered and threatened species are not the direct responsibility of the monument, coordination with agencies responsible for their welfare and recovery is necessary to ensure that activities taking place in the monument, and monument management, are effective in protecting and enhancing populations of those species. To support efforts to enhance protected species in the Northwestern Hawaiian Islands, the monument has identified two strategies for achieving this goal:

- Coordinate with partners on protected species needs by communicating regularly with jurisdictional agencies on protected species issues and assisting in the development and implementation of a protected species threat reduction assessment for the Northwestern Hawaiian Islands.

- Support and facilitate research on protected species by identifying research needs and supporting research to enhance populations of protected species and incorporating new data on candidate and protected species into the Northwestern Hawaiian Islands biogeographic assessment database.

Maritime Archaeological Resources

Proposed strategies and associated activities in the monument action plan are designed to increase our understanding of maritime heritage resources and foster effective and protective management in the monument. These strategies are as follows:

- Document and inventory maritime heritage resources. Preserving and appreciating maritime heritage resources begins with documentary research and field inventory surveys. These activities are similar to those associated with ecosystem research. Both involve consolidation of past information, diving operations, and mapping or remote sensing surveys. Maritime heritage field surveys are therefore compatible with multidisciplinary research missions.

- Incorporate maritime heritage into public education and outreach. Raising public awareness of the maritime heritage field is essential to better valuing and protecting the resource. Protection comes through understanding the nature of maritime heritage resources, as well as familiarity with established preservation efforts. Education and outreach for maritime resources emphasize "bringing the place to the people, not the people to the place" in a responsible manner.

- Coordinate monument agency efforts to protect maritime heritage resources. Because of NOAA's previous maritime heritage work in the region, efforts to inventory, evaluate, interpret and preserve maritime heritage resources in the Northwestern Hawaiian Islands will be coordinated from the Pacific Islands regional office by NOAA maritime heritage staff and conducted in close collaboration and coordination between NOAA, the Hawaii Department of Land and Natural Resources and U.S. Fish and Wildlife Service. Each program or agency provides expertise in the joint preservation of these non-renewable resources.

Existing NOAA and U.S. Fish and Wildlife Service Monument Regulations

Except where necessary to respond to emergencies threatening life, property, or the environment or activities necessary for law enforcement purposes or armed forces actions, the following activities are prohibited throughout the monument:

- Removing, moving, taking, harvesting, possessing, injuring, disturbing, or damaging; or attempting to remove, move, take, harvest, possess, injure, disturb, or damage any living or nonliving monument resource (71 FR 51134).

State and Federal Preservation Laws

A number of established laws govern the protection and management of maritime heritage resources. The Abandoned Shipwreck Act of 1987 charges each state with the preservation management for "certain abandoned shipwrecks, which have been deserted and to which the owner has relinquished ownership rights with no retention." In the State of Hawaii the preservation and protection of historic properties on state submerged lands falls under HRS Chapter 6E, which established the State Historic Preservation Program. For both NOAA and U.S. Fish and Wildlife Service, preservation mandates for maritime heritage resources derive directly from elements of the Federal Archaeology Program, including the National Historic Preservation Act of 1966. Section

110 of the Act states that each federal agency shall establish a preservation program for the protection of historic properties. Other relevant preservation guidelines include the Antiquities Act of 1906, Archaeological Resources Protection Act of 1979, National Environmental Policy Act of 1982, the Preserve America Executive Order (EO 13287 2003), and the Sunken Military Craft Act of 2004. These laws codify the protection of heritage sites from illegal salvage and looting. NOAA's Maritime Heritage Program and the monument's Maritime Heritage Action Plan are specifically designed to address these preservation mandates and both inventory and protect these special resources for the benefit of the public.

Native Hawaiian Cultural Resources

Native Hawaiian practices exercised for subsistence and other cultural purposes are based on a value system that is consistent with resource protection and preservation and serve as long-term conservation measures. The monument has identified a strategy and associated activities to support Native Hawaiian subsistence, cultural and religious practices in the Northwestern Hawaiian Islands:

■ Review Native Hawaiian practices permit applications and track and monitor permitted activities.

■ Support Native Hawaiian practices by: supporting Native Hawaiian cultural research and education; developing outreach for those planning expeditions for Native Hawaiian practices; and seeking assistance from permittees to share lessons learned from their experiences.

Understanding the Northwestern Hawaiian Islands from a Native Hawaiian perspective benefits the monument in many ways. Native Hawaiian research contributes to an ecosystem-based approach to management and complements other types of research. Education and outreach to the Native Hawaiian community can elicit greater involvement by Native Hawaiians in monument management. Utilizing cultural information in education and outreach will engage the broader public in learning about and caring for the Northwestern Hawaiian Islands. The monument has identified two strategies to increase understanding of Native Hawaiian histories and cultural practices related to the Northwestern Hawaiian Islands:

■ Support Native Hawaiian cultural and historical research by: identifying cultural research needs and priorities; supporting Native Hawaiian cultural research of the Northwestern Hawaiian Islands; identifying ways of integrating Native Hawaiian traditional ecological knowledge and management concepts into monument management, and; seeking protective status, as appropriate, to protect cultural sites.

■ Provide cultural outreach and educational opportunities to the Native Hawaiian community and the general public by: integrating Native Hawaiian values and cultural information into a general outreach and education program; developing a culturally based strategy for education and outreach to the Native Hawaiian community; integrating Native Hawaiian values and cultural information into a monument permittee education and outreach program; and facilitating cultural education opportunities in the field for students, teachers and cultural specialists.

Concluding Remarks

This initial report on resource status and trends for the Papahānaumokuākea Marine National Monument indicates the need for management actions that address potential impacts of key habitats, degrading conditions of some living resources (Hawaiian Monk seals, resident seabirds and migratory shorebirds), a general need to increase knowledge of regional biodiversity, and enhanced research and discovery of marine archaeological resources. Although the Northwestern Hawaiian Islands are often referred to as remote and relatively pristine, only seven of the seventeen categories received the highest rating of good. The factors contributing to these slightly diminished rankings suggest areas of focus for management actions, including marine debris, the health of threatened and endangered species, and research on the impacts of climate change. Only three categories were rated as fair (the lowest ranking assigned to any of the categories for the Northwestern Hawaiian Islands), suggesting that the overall condition of these ecosystems is good relative to the more heavily impacted reefs of the main Hawaiian Islands.

Although the monument currently limits permitted human activity, Midway Atoll is open to a limited number of visitors. The Midway Atoll Visitor Service Action Plan, a section of the recently completed Monument Management Plan, guides visitor activities. Visitor activities, when possible, assist with management and conservation activities the Northwestern Hawaiian Islands.

Archeological resources in the monument are an important link to the history of this area. Loss of these resources by natural processes is difficult to mitigate. In order to preserve the artifacts and history, it is therefore important to identify, locate and document these resources.

An important focus of the monument will be to continue to recognize and perpetuate the unique relationship of native Hawaiians to the land, sea and their cultural traditions. The monument can facilitate this relationship by serving as a catalyst for strengthening the bond between the Hawaiian people and the lands and waters of the Northwestern Hawaiian Islands. Incorporating traditional values and ecological knowledge into the natural resource management of the Northwestern Hawaiian Islands will be an important part of all management initiatives in this region.

Acknowledgements

Clancy Environmental Consultants, Inc., under contract to NOAA, was instrumental in developing the template for this document and providing the initial material. We would particularly like to thank Jeff Rosen for developing the condition summary table and Karen Fox for drafting content. We thank our reviewers for their helpful comments: Dr. Jo-Ann Leong (Hawaii Institute of Marine Biology), Sam Pooley (Pacific Islands Fisheries Science Center) and Dan Polhemus (Hawaii State Department of Land and Natural Resources and the Bishop Museum).

Cited Resources

Aeby, G.S. 2006. Baseline levels of coral disease in the Northwestern Hawaiian Islands. Paper read at the Northwestern Hawaiian Islands 3rd Scientific Symposium, Honolulu.

Angermeier, P.L. and J.R. Karr, 1994. Biological integrity versus biological diversitynas policy directives: Protecting biotic resources. BioScience 44:690-697.

Antonelis, G.A., J.D. Baker, T.C. Johanos, R.C. Braun and A.L. Harting. 2004. Hawaiian monk seal (*Monachus schauinslandi*): status and conservation issues. Atoll Res. Bull. 543:75-101.

Baker, J.D., C.L. Littnan ,D.W. Johnston. 2006. Potential effects of sea level rise on the terrestrial habitats of endangered and endemic megafauna in the Northwestern Hawaiian Islands. Endangered Species Research 2:21-30. http://www.int-res.com/articles/esr2006/2/n002p021.pdf

Balazs, G.H. and M. Chaloupka. 2003. Thirty-year recovery trend in the once depleted Hawaiian green sea turtle stock. Biol. Conserv. 117:491–498.

Bertilsson-Friedman, P.A. 2002. Shark inflicted injuries to the endangered Hawaiian monk seal, *Monachus schauinslandi*. M.S. Thesis, University of New Hampshire. 91 pp.

Carretta, J.V., K.A. Forney, M.S. Lowry, J. Barlow, J. Baker, D. Johnston, B. Hanson, M.M. Muto. 2008. Draft U.S. Pacific marine mammal stock assessments: 2008. NOAA Technical Memorandum NMFS-SWFSC-XXX, U.S. Department of Commerce. http://www.nmfs.noaa.gov/pr/sars/draft.htm

Census of Coral Reef Ecosystems (CReefs). 2006 French Frigate Shoals Cruise. A project of the Census of Marine Life. http://www.creefs.org/

Clague, D.A. 1996. The growth and subsidence of the Hawaiian-Emperor volcanic chain. In: Keast A., S.D. Miller (eds.) The origin and evolution of the Pacific Island biotas, New Guinea to eastern Polynesia: patterns and processes. SPB Academic Publishing, Amsterdam, pp 35-50.

Clapp, R.B. and R.W. Woodward. 1972. The natural history of Kure Atoll, NWHI. Atoll Res. Bull. 164:303-304.

Cleghorn, Paul. 1988. The settlement and abandonment of two Hawaiian outposts: Nihoa and Necker Islands. Bishop Museum occasional papers Vol. 28, pp. 35-49.

Craig, M.P. and T.J. Ragan. 1999. Body size, survival, and decline of juvenile Hawaiian monk seals, *Monachus schauinslandi*. Mar. Mammal Sci. 15(3):786-809.

Dameron O.J., M. Parke, M. Albins, R. Brainard. 2007. Marine debris accumulation in the Northwestern Hawaiian Islands: An examination of rates and processes. Mar. Poll. Bull. 54(4):423-433.

David, M., S. Campbell, L.A. Woodward, Q.X. Li. 2001. Characterization of a carbofuran-contaminated site in the Hawaiian Islands National Wildlife Refuge. In: J.J. Johnston (ed.) Pesticides and Wildlife: ACS Symposium Series 771. Chapter 3:22-37.

DiNardo, G.T. and R. Marshall. 2001. Status of Lobster Stocks in the Northwestern Hawaiian Islands, 1998-2000. Southwest Fisheries Science Center, Administrative Report, H-01-04.

Eldredge, L.G. and S.E. Miller. 1994. Records of the Hawaii Biological Survey for 1994. Bishop Museum Occasional Papers 41:3-18.

Emory, K. 1928. Archaeology of Nihoa and Necker. Bishop Museum Bulletin 53. Honolulu, Bishop Museum Press.

Firing, J.B., R. Brainard, E. Firing. 2004. Ten years of shipboard ADCP measurements along the Northwestern Hawaiian Islands. In: Northwestern Hawaiian Islands: 3rd Scientific Symposium, Honolulu. 18 pp.

Friedlander, A.M. and E.E. DeMartini. 2002. Contrasts in density, size, and biomass of reef fishes between the northwestern and the main Hawaiian islands: the effects of fishing down apex predators. Mar. Ecol-Prog. Ser. 230:253-264.

Friedlander, A.M., G. Aeby, R. Brainard, A. Clark, E. DeMartini, S. Godwin, J. Kenyon, R. Kosaki, J. Maragos, P. Vroom. 2005. The sate of coral reef ecosystems of the Northwestern Hawaiian Islands. pp. 270-311. In: J. Waddell (ed.), The state of coral reef ecosystems of the United States and Pacific freely associated states: 2005. NOAA Technical Memorandum, NOS NCCOS 11. NOAA/NCCOS Center for Coastal Monitoring and Assessment's Biogeography Team. Silver Spring, MD. 522 pp. http://ccma.nos.noaa.gov/ecosystems/coralreef/coral_report_2005/NWHI_Ch10_C.pdf

Garrison, T. 1999. Oceanography: an invitation to marine science, 3rd ed. Wadsworth Publishing Co. Belt, CA.

Gilmartin, W.G. 1993. Research and management plan for the Hawaiian monk seal at French Frigate Shoals, 1993-96. Honolulu Lab., Southwest Fisheries Science Center, Natl. Marine Fish. Serv., Admin. Rept. H-93-08. 22 pp.

Gilmartin, W.G., R.L. DeLong, A.W. Smith, L.A. Griner, M.D. Dailey. 1980. An investigation into unusual mortality in the Hawaiian monk seal, *Monachus schauinslandi.* In: Grigg, R.W. and R.T. Pfund (eds.). Proceedings of the Symposium on Status of Resource Investigation in the Northwestern Hawaiian Islands, April 24-25, 1980, p 32-41. Univ. HI, Sea Grant Rept. UNIHI-SEAGRANT-MR-80-04.

Godwin, S., K. Rodgers, P. Jokiel. 2005. Reducing potential impact of invasive marine species in the Northwestern Hawaiian Islands Marine National Monument. Hawai'i Coral Reef Assessment and Monitoring Program (CRAMP) Hawai'i Institute of Marine Biology. http://cramp.wcc.hawaii.edu/CRAMP_Information/publications.htm

Harvell, C., K. Kim, J. Burkholder, R. Colwell, P. Epstein, D. Grimes, E. Hofmann, E. Lipp, A. Osterhaus, R. Over-street, J. Porter, G. Smith, G. Vasta. 1999. Emerging Marine Diseases – climate links and anthropogenic factors. Science 285:1505-1510. http://chge.med.harvard.edu/publications/journals/documents/harvell.pdf

Henderson, J.R. 2001. A pre- and post-MARPOL Annex V summary of Hawaiian monk seal entanglements and marine debris accumulation in the Northwestern Hawaiian Islands, 1982-1998. Mar. Poll. Bull. 42:584-589.

Herman, L.M. 1979. Humpback whales in Hawaiian waters: A study in historical ecology. Pac. Sci. 33:1-15.

Hoeke, R., R. Brainard, R. Moffitt, M. Merrifield. 2006. The role of oceanographic conditions and reef morphology in the 2002 coral bleaching event in the Northwestern Hawaiian Islands. Atoll Res. Bull. 543:489-503. http://www.pifsc.noaa.gov/library/pubs/HoekeARB543_Final.pdf

Johnston, D.W., M.E. Chapla, L.E. Williams, D.K. Mattila. 2007. Identification of humpback whale *Megaptera novaengliae* wintering habitat in the Northwestern Hawaiian Islands using spatial habitat modeling. Endangered Species Research 3:249-257.

Jokiel, P.L. and E. Brown. 2004. Global warming, regional trends and inshore environmental conditions influence coral bleaching in Hawaii. Glob. Change Biol. 10(10):1627-1641.

Kelley, C. and R. Moffit. 2004. The impacts of bottomfishing on the Raita and West St. Rogatien Reserve Preservation Areas in the Northwestern Hawaiian Islands Coral Reef Ecosystem Reserve. Unpublished report, Hawaii Undersea Research Laboratory, 49 pp.

Kenyon, K.W. 1972. Man versus the monk seal. J. Mammalogy 53(4):687-696.

Kenyon J.C. and R.E. Brainard. 2006. Second recorded episode of mass coral bleaching in the Northwestern Hawaiian Islands. Atoll Res. Bull. 543:505-523.

Kenyon J.C., G.S. Aeby, R.E. Brainard, J.D. Chojnacki, M.J. Dunlap, C.B. Wilkinson. 2006. Mass coral bleaching on high-latitude reefs in the Hawaiian Archipelago. In: Y. Suzuki, T. Nakamori, M. Hidaka, H. Kayanne, B.E. Cassareto, K. Nadooka, H. Yamano, M. Tsuchiya (eds.) Proceedings of the 10th International Coral Reef Symposium Okinawa, Japan. 1950 pp.

Kikiloi, S. 2006. Reconnecting with Ancestral Islands: Examining historical relationships between kānaka maoli and the Northwestern Hawaiian Islands. Report to NOAA for the Kia'i Kai [Guardians of the Sea] Project, Kamakakūokalani, Center for Hawaiian Studies U.H. Mānoa, January.

Kleypas, J. A., R.A. Feely, V. J. Fabry, C. Langdon, C.L. Sabine, L.L. Robbins. 2006. Impacts of Ocean Acidification on Coral Reefs and Other Marine Calcifiers: A Guide for Future Research, report of a workshop held 18-20 April 2005, St. Petersburg, FL, sponsored by NSF, NOAA and the U.S. Geological Survey, 88 pp.

Kushlan, J. A., M.J. Steinkamp, K.C. Parsons, J. Capp, M. Acosta Cruz, M. Coulter, I. Davidson, L. Dickson, N. Edelson, R. Elliot, R.M. Erwin, S. Hatch, S. Kress, R. Milko, S. Miller, K. Mills, R. Paul, R. Phillips, J.E. Saliva, B. Sydeman, J. Trapp, J. Wheeler, K. Wohl. 2002. Waterbird conservation for the Americas: The North American waterbird conservation plan, version 1. Washington, D.C.: Waterbird Conservation for the Americas. 78 pp.

Mantua, N.J., S.R. Hare, Y. Zhang, J.M. Wallace, R.C. Francis. 1997. A Pacific interdecadal climate oscillation with impacts on salmon production. B. Am. Meteorol. Soc. 78:1069-1079.

Maragos, J.E., D.C. Potts, G. Aeby, D. Gulko, J. Kenyon, D. Siciliano, D. VanRavenswaay. 2004. 2000-2002 rapid ecological assessment of corals (Anthozoa) on shallow reefs of the Northwester Hawaiian Islands. Part 1. Species and distribution. Pac. Sci. 58(2):211-230.

Miao, X.S., L. Woodward, C. Swenson, Q.X. Li. 2001. Comparative concentrations of metals in marine species from French Frigate Shoals, North Pacific Ocean. Mar. Poll. Bull. 42(11):1049-1054.

Miller, S.E. and L.G. Eldredge. 1996. Numbers of Hawaiian species: Supplement 1. Bishop Museum Occasional Papers 45:8-17.

National Marine Fisheries Service and U.S. Fish and Wildlife Service (USFWS). 1998. Recovery plan for U.S. Pacific populations of the green turtle (*Chelonia mydas*). National Marine Fisheries Service, Silver Spring, MD. http://www.nmfs.noaa.gov/pr/pdfs/recovery/turtle_green_pacific.pdf

National Marine Fisheries Service (NMFS). 2005. Stock assessment of the Hawaiian monk seal. http://www.nmfs.noaa.gov/pr/pdfs/sars/po2005sehm-hi.pdf

National Marine Fisheries Service (NMFS). 2006. Recovery plan for the Hawaiian monk seal (*Monachus schauinslandi*). National Marine Fisheries Service, Silver Spring, MD. 154 pp. http://www.nmfs.noaa.gov/pr/pdfs/recovery/draft_hawaiianmonkseal.pdf

National Marine Fisheries Service (NMFS). 2007. Recovery Plan for the Hawaiian Monk Seal (*Monachus schauinslandi*). Second Revision. National Marine Fisheries Service, Silver Spring, MD. 165 pp.

National Marine Sanctuary Program (NMSP). 2004a. A monitoring framework for the National Marine Sanctuary System. U.S. Dept. of Commerce, National Oceanic and Atmospheric Administration, National Ocean Service. Silver Spring, MD. 22 pp.

National Marine Sanctuary Program (NMSP). 2004b. Advice and recommendations on development of draft fishing regulations under the National Marine Sanctuaries Act Section 304(a)(5) for the proposed Northwestern Hawaiian Islands National Marine Sanctuary. http://hawaiireef.noaa.gov/designation/pdfs/Final_NMSA_304a5.pdf

National Marine Sanctuary Program (NMSP). 2005. Northwestern Hawaiian Islands coral reef ecosystem reserve final reserve operations plan. 255 pp. http://hawaiireef.noaa.gov/PDFs/Final_ROP.pdf

National Oceanic and Atmospheric Administration (NOAA). 1998 (on-line). The extent and condition of U.S. coral reefs" by Steven L. Miller and Michael P. Crosby. NOAA's State of the Coast Report. Silver Spring, MD: NOAA. http://oceanservice.noaa.gov/websites/retiredsites/sotc_pdf/CRF.PDF

National Ocean Service (NOS). 2003. Atlas of the Shallow-Water Benthic Habitats of the Northwestern Hawaiian Islands. http://ccma.nos.noaa.gov/products/coast/pdf/Atlas_sec1.pdf

Parrish, F.A., K. Abernathy, G.J. Marshall, B.M. Buhleiert. 2002. Hawaiian monk seals (*Monachus schauinslandi*) foraging in deep-water coral beds. Mar. Mammal Sci. 18(1):244-248.

Polovina, J.J., G.T. Mitchum, N.E. Graham, M.P. Craig, E.E. DeMartini, E.N. Flint. 1994. Physical and biological consequences of a climate event in the central North Pacific. Fish Oceanogr. 3:5-21.

Quackenbush, S. L., R.N. Casey, R.J. Murcek, T.A. Paul, T.M. Work, C.J. Limpus, A. Chaves, L. duToit, J. Vasconcelos, A.A. Aguirre, T.R. Spraker, J.A. Horrocks, L.A. Vermeer, G.H. Balazs and J.W. Casey. 2001. Quantitative analysis of herpesvirus sequences from normal tissue and fibropapillomas of marine turtles with real-time PCR. Virology 287:105-111.

Randall, J.E. 1987. Introductions of marine fishes to the Hawaiian Islands. B. Mar. Sci. 41: 490-502.

Randall, J.E. 1992. Endemism of fishes in Oceania. UNEP Regional Seas Rep. Studl 147:55-67.

Seki, M.P., J.J. Polovina, D.R. Kobayashi, R.R. Bidigare, G.T. Mitchum. 2002. An oceanographic characterization of swordfish longline fishing grounds in the Subtropical North Pacific. Fish Oceanogr. 11 (5): 251-266. http://www.pifsc.noaa.gov/eod/pub/FOG_Seki-etal-02.pdf

Sharp W.D. and D.A. Clague. 2006. 50-Ma initiation of Hawaii-Emperor bend records major change in Pacific plate motion. Science 313:1281–1284

Sileo, L., P.R. Sievert, M.D. Samuel. 1990. Causes of mortality of albatross chicks at Midway Atoll. J Wildlife Dis 26:329-338.

State of Hawai'i, Department of Land and Natural Resources, Division of Aquatic Resources. 2003. Aquatic Invasive Species Management Plan. http://www.state.hi.us/dlnr/dar/pubs/ais_mgmt_plan_final.pdf

Turgeon, D., M. Harmon, K. McMahon. 2002. Contaminants. In: J. Maragos and D. Gulko (eds.), p. 44, Coral reef ecosystems of the North-western Hawaiian Islands: Interim results emphasizing the 2000 surveys. Maragos, J. and D. Gulko (eds.). U.S. Fish and Wildlife Service and the Hawaii Department of Land and Natural Resources, Honolulu, Hawaii, 46 pp. http://coastalscience.noaa.gov/documents/nowramp.pdf

U.S. Fish and Wildlife Service (USFWS). 2000. National Marine Fisheries Service and Department of Land and Natural Resources.Press release.

U.S. Fish and Wildlife Service (USFWS). 2006. Interim visitor services plan, midway atoll national wildlife refuge. (U.S. Fish and Wildlife Service 2006 http://www.fws.gov/midway/vsp.html

Van Tilburg, H. 2002. Maritime Cultural Resources Survey: Northwestern Hawaiian Islands/, submitted to NWHI Coral Reef Ecosystem Reserve.

Vatter, A. 2003. Bottom longline fishing for sharks in the Northwestern Hawaiian Islands. National Marine Fisheries Service Pacific Islands Region Administrative Report ARPIR- 03-01.

Wessel P., Y. Harada, L.W. Kroenke. 2006. Towards a self-consistent, high-resolution absolute plate motion model for the Pacific. Geochemistry, Geophysics, Geosystems 7. 7, Q03L12, doi:10.1029/2005GC001000

Western Pacific Regional Fishery Management Council (WPRFMC). 1986. Combined fishery management plan, environmental assessment, and regulatory impact review for the bottomfish and seamount groundfish fisheries of the western pacific region. Honolulu, Hawaii. 314 pp.

Western Pacific Regional Fishery Management Council (WPRFMC). 2001. Final fishery management plan for the coral reef ecosystems of the western Pacific region, vol. 1. Honolulu.

Western Pacific Regional Fishery Management Council (WPRFMC). 2003. Managing U.S. fisheries of the U.S. Pacific Islands: past, present and future. NOAA Award Number NA03NMF4410053.

Western Pacific Regional Fishery Management Council (WPRFMC) 2004. Bottomfish and seamount groundfish fisheries of the Western Pacific region. 2002 Annual Report. Honolulu, Hawaii.

Western Pacific Regional Fishery Management Council (WPRFMC). 2006. Draft amendments to the fishery management plans of the Western Pacific region regarding fishing activities in the proposed Northwestern Hawaiian Islands Sanctuary.http://www.wpcouncil.org/NWHI/Documents/2006CombinedNWHIAmendments-04032006.pdf

White, D. 2007. Ciguatoxin characterization in Hawaiian archipelago fishes: toxicity identified by N2A bioassay. Masters thesis, Univ. of Hawaii at Hilo.

Work, T., G. Balaz, R. Rameyer, R. Morris. 2004. Retrospective pathology survey of green turtles (*Chelonia mydas*) with fibropapillomatosis from the Hawaiian Islands, 1993-2003. Dis. Aquat. Organ.Organisms 62:163-176.

Work, T.M. G.S. Aeby, S.L. Coles. 2008. Distribution and morphology of growth anomalies in Acropora from the Indo—Pacific. Dis. Aquat. Organ. 78(3):255-264.

Additional Resources

Antiquities Act of 1906: http://www.cr.nps.gov/history/hisnps/npshistory/antiq.htm

Abandoned Shipwreck Act of 1987: http://www.nps.gov/archeology/tools/Laws/ASA.htm

Bishop Museum: http://www.bishopmuseum.org

Coral-List Web site, 2004 coral bleaching in the Northwestern Hawaiian Islands: http://coral.aoml.noaa.gov/pipermail/coral-list/2004-October/001390.html

Endangered Species Act: http://www.nmfs.noaa.gov/pr/laws/esa

Hawai'i Coral Reef Initiative Research Program: www.hawaii.edu/ssri/hcri

Hawai'i Institute of Marine Biology: http://www.hawaii.edu/HIMB

Marine Conservation Biology Institute: http://www.mcbi.org

Marine Mammal Protection Act of 1972: http://www.nmfs.noaa.gov/pr/laws/mmpa

Marine Protected Areas of the United States: http://www.mpa.gov

Migratory Bird Treaty Act of 1918: http://www.fws.gov/laws/lawsdigest/migtrea.html

National Historic Preservation Act of 1966: http://www.cr.nps.gov/local-law/nhpa1966.htm

Naval Historical Center: http://www.history.navy.mil

National Park Service: http://www.nps.gov

NOAA Coral Reef Conservation Program: http://www.coralreef.noaa.gov

NOAA Coral Reef Information System (CoRIS): http://www.coris.noaa.gov

NOAA Marine Debris Program: http://marinedebris.noaa.gov

NOAA National Marine Fisheries Service: http://www.nmfs.noaa.gov

NOAA National Marine Fisheries Service Office of Protected Resources: http://www.nmfs.noaa.gov/pr

NOAA National Marine Fisheries Service Draft Marine Mammal Stock Assessment Reports: http://www.nmfs.noaa.gov/pr/sars/draft.htm

NOAA National Marine Fisheries Service Pacific Islands Fisheries Science Center: http://www.pifsc.noaa.gov

NOAA National Marine Fisheries Service, Pacific Islands Fisheries Science Center, Bottomfish Research and Stock Assessment: http://www.pifsc.noaa.gov/bottomfish

NOAA Office of National Marine Sanctuaries: http://sanctuaries.noaa.gov

NOAA Ocean Explorer: http://www.oceanexplorer.noaa.gov

Northwestern Hawaiian Islands Marine National Monument. A Citizen's Guide: http://hawaiireef.noaa.gov/PDFs/Citizens_Guide_Web.pdf

Northwestern Hawaiian Islands Multi-Agency Education Project Web site, French frigate shoals: http://www.hawaiianatolls.org/about/ffs.php

Papahānaumokuākea Marine National Monument: http://hawaiireef.noaa.gov

Papahānaumokuākea Marine National Monument Management Plan: http://www.hawaiireef.noaa.gov/management/mp.html

State of Hawaii: http://www.hawaii.gov

State of Hawaii's Department of Land and Natural Resources: http://hawaii.gov/dlnr

Sunken Military Craft Act: http://www.history.navy.mil/branches/org12-12a.htm

The White House Web site, Establishment of the Northwestern Hawaiian Islands Marine National Monument: http://www.whitehouse.gov/news/releases/2006/06/20060615-18.html

U.S. Fish and Wildlife Service: http://www.fws.gov

U.S. Geological Survey: http://www.usgs.gov

U.S. Geological Survey, The Long Trail of the Hawaiian Hotspot: http://pubs.usgs.gov/gip/dynamic/Hawaiian.html

Western Pacific Fishery Management Council: http://www.wpcouncil.org

Woods Hole Oceanographic Institution: http://www.whoi.edu

Appendix A: Rating Scheme for System-Wide Monitoring Questions

The purpose of this appendix is to clarify the 17 questions and possible responses used to report the condition of sanctuary resources in "Condition Reports" for all national marine sanctuaries. Individual staff and partners utilized this guidance, as well as their own informed and detailed understanding of the site to make judgments about the status and trends of sanctuary resources.

The questions derive from the National Marine Sanctuary System's mission, and a system-wide monitoring framework (National Marine Sanctuary Program 2004) developed to ensure the timely flow of data and information to those responsible for managing and protecting resources in the ocean and coastal zone, and to those that use, depend on and study the ecosystems encompassed by the sanctuaries. They are being used to guide staff and partners at each of the 14 sites in the sanctuary system in the development of this first periodic sanctuary condition report. Evaluations of status and trends may be based on interpretation of quantitative and, when necessary, non-quantitative assessments and observations of scientists, managers and users.

Judging an ecosystem as having "integrity" implies the relative wholeness of ecosystem structure, function, and associated complexity, along with the spatial and temporal variability inherent in these characteristics, as determined by its natural evolutionary history. Ecosystem integrity is reflected in the system's "ability to generate and maintain adaptive biotic elements through natural evolutionary process" (Angermeier and Karr 1994). The natural fluctuations of a system's native characteristics, including abiotic drivers, biotic composition, complex relationships, and functional processes are unaltered and are either likely to persist or be regained following natural disturbance.

Following a brief discussion about each question, statements are presented that were used to judge the status and assign a corresponding color code. These statements are customized for each question. In addition, the following options are available for all questions: " N/A" - the question does not apply; and "Undet." - resource status is undetermined.

Symbols used to indicate trends are the same for all questions: "▲ " - conditions appear to be improving; "—" - conditions do not appear to be changing; "▼ " - conditions appear to be declining; and "?" – trend is undetermined.

Water Stressors

1. | **Question 1 (Water/Stressors): Are specific or multiple stressors, including changing oceanographic and atmospheric conditions, affecting water quality and how are they changing?**

This is meant to capture shifts in condition arising from certain changing physical processes and anthropogenic inputs. Factors resulting in regionally accelerated rates of change in water temperature, salinity, dissolved oxygen or water clarity could all be judged to reduce water quality. Localized changes in circulation or sedimentation resulting, for example, from coastal construction or dredge spoil disposal can affect light penetration, salinity regimes, oxygen levels, productivity, waste transport and other factors that influence habitat and living resource quality. Human inputs, generally in the form of contaminants from point or nonpoint sources, including fertilizers, pesticides, hydrocarbons, heavy metals and sewage, are common causes of environmental degradation, often in combination rather than alone. Certain biotoxins, such as domoic acid, may be of particular interest to specific sanctuaries. When present in the water column, any of these contaminants can affect marine life by direct contact or ingestion, or through bioaccumulation via the food chain.

[Note: Over time, accumulation in sediments can sequester and concentrate contaminants. Their effects may manifest only when the sediments are resuspended during storm or other energetic events. In such cases, reports of status should be made under Question 7 – Habitat contaminants.]

Good	Conditions do not appear to have the potential to negatively affect living resources or habitat quality.
Good/Fair	Selected conditions may preclude full development of living resource assemblages and habitats, but are not likely to cause substantial or persistent declines.
Fair	Selected conditions may inhibit the development of assemblages and may cause measurable but not severe declines in living resources and habitats.
Fair/Poor	Selected conditions have caused or are likely to cause severe declines in some but not all living resources and habitats.
Poor	Selected conditions have caused or are likely to cause severe declines in most, if not all, living resources and habitats.

Water
Eutrophic
Condition

2. | **What is the eutrophic condition of sanctuary waters and how is it changing?**

Nutrient enrichment often leads to planktonic and/or benthic algae blooms. Some affect benthic communities directly through space competition. Overgrowth and other competitive interactions (e.g., accumulation of algal-sediment mats) often lead to shifts in dominance in the benthic assemblage. Disease incidence and frequency can also be affected by algae competition and the resulting chemistry along competitive boundaries. Blooms can also affect water column conditions, including light penetration and plankton availability, which can alter pelagic food webs. Harmful algal blooms often affect resources, as biotoxins are released into the water and air, and oxygen can be depleted.

Good	Conditions do not appear to have the potential to negatively affect living resources or habitat quality.
Good/Fair	Selected conditions may preclude full development of living resource assemblages and habitats, but are not likely to cause substantial or persistent declines.
Fair	Selected conditions may inhibit the development of assemblages and may cause measurable but not severe declines in living resources and habitats.
Fair/Poor	Selected conditions have caused or are likely to cause severe declines in some but not all living resources and habitats.
Poor	Selected conditions have caused or are likely to cause severe declines in most if not all living resources and habitats.

Water
Human Health

3. | **Do sanctuary waters pose risks to human health and how are they changing?**

Human health concerns are generally aroused by evidence of contamination (usually bacterial or chemical) in bathing waters or fish intended for consumption. They also emerge when harmful algal blooms are reported or when cases of respiratory distress or other disorders attributable to harmful algal blooms increase dramatically. Any of these conditions should be considered in the course of judging the risk to humans posed by waters in a marine sanctuary.

Some sites may have access to specific information on beach and shellfish conditions. In particular, beaches may be closed when criteria for safe water body contact are exceeded, or shellfish harvesting may be prohibited when contaminant loads or infection rates exceed certain levels. These conditions can be evaluated in the context of the descriptions below.

Good	Conditions do not appear to have the potential to negatively affect human health.
Good/Fair	Selected conditions that have the potential to affect human health may exist but human impacts have not been reported.
Fair	Selected conditions have resulted in isolated human impacts, but evidence does not justify widespread or persistent concern.
Fair/Poor	Selected conditions have caused or are likely to cause severe impacts, but cases to date have not suggested a pervasive problem.
Poor	Selected conditions warrant widespread concern and action, as large-scale, persistent and/or repeated severe impacts are likely or have occurred.

Water
Human Activities

4. | **What are the levels of human activities that may influence water quality and how are they changing?**

Among the human activities in or near sanctuaries that affect water quality are those involving direct discharges (transiting vessels, visiting vessels, onshore and offshore industrial facilities, public wastewater facilities), those that contribute contaminants to stream, river, and water control discharges (agriculture, runoff from impermeable surfaces through storm drains, conversion of land use), and those releasing airborne chemicals that subsequently deposit via particulates at sea (vessels, land-based traffic, power plants, manufacturing facilities, refineries). In addition, dredging and trawling can cause resuspension of contaminants in sediments.

Good   Few or no activities occur that are likely to negatively affect water quality.

Good/Fair Some potentially harmful activities exist, but they do not appear to have had a negative effect on water quality.

Fair   Selected activities have resulted in measurable resource impacts, but evidence suggests effects are localized, not widespread.

Fair/Poor Selected activities have caused or are likely to cause severe impacts, and cases to date suggest a pervasive problem.

Poor   Selected activities warrant widespread concern and action, as large-scale, persistent, and/or repeated severe impacts have occurred or are likely to occur.

Habitat
Abundance & Distribution

5. | **What are the abundance and distribution of major habitat types and how are they changing?**

Habitat loss is of paramount concern when it comes to protecting marine and terrestrial ecosystems. Of greatest concern to sanctuaries are changes caused, either directly or indirectly, by human activities. The loss of shoreline is recognized as a problem indirectly caused by human activities. Habitats with submerged aquatic vegetation are often altered by changes in water conditions in estuaries, bays, and nearshore waters. Intertidal zones can be affected for long periods by spills or by chronic pollutant exposure. Beaches and haul-out areas can be littered with dangerous marine debris, as can the water column or benthic habitats. Sandy subtidal areas and hardbottoms are frequently disturbed or destroyed by trawling. Even rocky areas several hundred meters deep are increasingly affected by certain types of trawls, bottom longlines and fish traps. Groundings, anchors and divers damage submerged reefs. Cables and pipelines disturb corridors across numerous habitat types and can be destructive if they become mobile. Shellfish dredging removes, alters and fragments habitats.

The result of these activities is the gradual reduction of the extent and quality of marine habitats. Losses can often be quantified through visual surveys and to some extent using high-resolution mapping. This question asks about the quality of habitats compared to those that would be expected without human impacts. The status depends on comparison to a baseline that existed in the past - one toward which restoration efforts might aim.

Good   Habitats are in pristine or near-pristine condition and are unlikely to preclude full community development.

Good/Fair Selected habitat loss or alteration has taken place, precluding full development of living resource assemblages, but it is unlikely to cause substantial or persistent degradation in living resources or water quality.

Fair   Selected habitat loss or alteration may inhibit the development of assemblages, and may cause measurable but not severe declines in living resources or water quality.

Fair/Poor Selected habitat loss or alteration has caused or is likely to cause severe declines in some but not all living resources or water quality.

Poor   Selected habitat loss or alteration has caused or is likely to cause severe declines in most if not all living resources or water quality.

Habitat Structure

6. | **What is the condition of biologically structured habitats and how is it changing?**

Many organisms depend on the integrity of their habitats and that integrity is largely determined by the condition of particular living organisms. Coral reefs may be the best known examples of such biologically-structured habitats. Not only is the substrate itself biogenic, but the diverse assemblages residing within and on the reefs depend on and interact with each other in tightly linked food webs. They also depend on each other for the recycling of wastes, hygiene and the maintenance of water quality, among other requirements.

Kelp beds may not be biogenic habitats to the extent of coral reefs, but kelp provides essential habitat for assemblages that would not reside or function together without it. There are other communities of organisms that are also similarly co-dependent, such as hard-bottom communities, which may be structured by bivalves, octocorals, coralline algae, or other groups that generate essential habitat for other species. Intertidal assemblages structured by mussels, barnacles, algae and seagrass beds are other examples. This question is intended to address these types of places where organisms form structures (habitats) on which other organisms depend.

■	**Good**	Habitats are in pristine or near-pristine condition and are unlikely to preclude full community development.
▨	**Good/Fair**	Selected habitat loss or alteration has taken place, precluding full development of living resources, but it is unlikely to cause substantial or persistent degradation in living resources or water quality.
	Fair	Selected habitat loss or alteration may inhibit the development of living resources and may cause measurable but not severe declines in living resources or water quality.
▨	**Fair/Poor**	Selected habitat loss or alteration has caused or is likely to cause severe declines in some but not all living resources or water quality.
■	**Poor**	Selected habitat loss or alteration has caused or is likely to cause severe declines in most if not all living resources or water quality.

Habitat Contaminants

7. | **What are the contaminant concentrations in sanctuary habitats and how are they changing?**

This question addresses the need to understand the risk posed by contaminants within benthic formations, such as soft sediments, hard bottoms, or biogenic organisms. In the first two cases, the contaminants can become available when released via disturbance. They can also pass upwards through the food chain after being ingested by bottom dwelling prey species. The contaminants of concern generally include pesticides, hydrocarbons and heavy metals, but the specific concerns of individual sanctuaries may differ substantially.

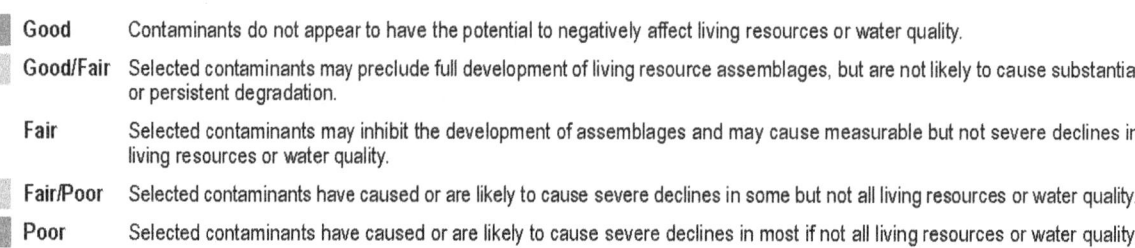

▨	**Good**	Contaminants do not appear to have the potential to negatively affect living resources or water quality.
▨	**Good/Fair**	Selected contaminants may preclude full development of living resource assemblages, but are not likely to cause substantial or persistent degradation.
	Fair	Selected contaminants may inhibit the development of assemblages and may cause measurable but not severe declines in living resources or water quality.
▨	**Fair/Poor**	Selected contaminants have caused or are likely to cause severe declines in some but not all living resources or water quality.
■	**Poor**	Selected contaminants have caused or are likely to cause severe declines in most if not all living resources or water quality.

Habitat
Human Activities

8. | **What are the levels of human activities that may influence habitat quality and how are they changing?**

Human activities that degrade habitat quality do so by affecting structural (geological), biological, oceanographic, acoustic or chemical characteristics. Structural impacts include removal or mechanical alteration, including various fishing techniques (trawls, traps, dredges, longlines and even hook-and-line in some habitats), dredging channels and harbors and dumping spoil, vessel groundings, anchoring, laying pipelines and cables, installing offshore structures, discharging drill cuttings, dragging tow cables, and placing artificial reefs. Removal or alteration of critical biological components of habitats can occur along with several of the above activities, most notably trawling, groundings and cable drags. Marine debris, particularly in large quantities (e.g., lost gill nets and other types of fishing gear), can affect both biological and structural habitat components. Changes in water circulation often occur when channels are dredged, fill is added, coastal areas are reinforced, or other construction takes place. These activities affect habitat by changing food delivery, waste removal, water quality (e.g., salinity, clarity and sedimentation), recruitment patterns and a host of other factors. Acoustic impacts can occur to water column habitats and organisms from acute and chronic sources of anthropogenic noise (e.g., shipping, boating, construction). Chemical alterations most commonly occur following spills and can have both acute and chronic impacts.

Good Few or no activities occur that are likely to negatively affect habitat quality.

Good/Fair Some potentially harmful activities exist, but they do not appear to have had a negative effect on habitat quality.

Fair Selected activities have resulted in measurable habitat impacts, but evidence suggests effects are localized, not widespread.

Fair/Poor Selected activities have caused or are likely to cause severe impacts, and cases to date suggest a pervasive problem.

Poor Selected activities warrant widespread concern and action, as large-scale, persistent and/or repeated severe impacts have occurred or are likely to occur.

Living Resources
Biodiversity

9. | **What is the status of biodiversity and how is it changing?**

This is intended to elicit thought and assessment of the condition of living resources based on expected biodiversity levels and the interactions between species. Intact ecosystems require that all parts not only exist, but that they function together, resulting in natural symbioses, competition and predator-prey relationships. Community integrity, resistance and resilience all depend on these relationships. Abundance, relative abundance, trophic structure, richness, H' diversity, evenness and other measures are often used to assess these attributes.

Good Biodiversity appears to reflect pristine or near-pristine conditions and promotes ecosystem integrity (full community development and function).

Good/Fair Selected biodiversity loss has taken place, precluding full community development and function, but it is unlikely to cause substantial or persistent degradation of ecosystem integrity.

Fair Selected biodiversity loss may inhibit full community development and function and may cause measurable but not severe degradation of ecosystem integrity.

Fair/Poor Selected biodiversity loss has caused or is likely to cause severe declines in some but not all ecosystem components and reduce ecosystem integrity.

Poor Selected biodiversity loss has caused or is likely to cause severe declines in ecosystem integrity.

Living Resources
Extracted Species

10. | What is the status of environmentally sustainable fishing and how is it changing?

Commercial and recreational harvesting are highly selective activities, for which fishers and collectors target a limited number of species, and often remove high proportions of populations. In addition to removing significant amounts of biomass from the ecosystem, reducing its availability to other consumers, these activities tend to disrupt specific and often critical food web links. When too much extraction occurs (i.e. ecologically unsustainable harvesting), trophic cascades ensue, resulting in changes in the abundance of non-targeted species as well. It also reduces the ability of the targeted species to replenish populations at a rate that supports continued ecosystem integrity.

It is essential to understand whether removals are occurring at ecologically sustainable levels. Knowing extraction levels and determining the impacts of removal are both ways that help gain this understanding. Measures for target species of abundance, catch amounts or rates (e.g., catch per unit effort), trophic structure and changes in non-target species abundance are all generally used to assess these conditions.

Other issues related to this question include whether fishers are using gear that is compatible with the habitats being fished and whether that gear minimizes by-catch and incidental take of marine mammals. For example, bottom-tending gear often destroys or alters both benthic structure and non-targeted animal and plant communities. "Ghost fishing" occurs when lost traps continue to capture organisms. Lost or active nets, as well as lines used to mark and tend traps and other fishing gear, can entangle marine mammals. Any of these could be considered indications of environmentally unsustainable fishing techniques.

Good	Extraction does not appear to affect ecosystem integrity (full community development and function).
Good/Fair	Extraction takes place, precluding full community development and function, but it is unlikely to cause substantial or persistent degradation of ecosystem integrity.
Fair	Extraction may inhibit full community development and function and may cause measurable but not severe degradation of ecosystem integrity.
Fair/Poor	Extraction has caused or is likely to cause severe declines in some but not all ecosystem components and reduce ecosystem integrity.
Poor	Extraction has caused or is likely to cause severe declines in ecosystem integrity.

Living Resources
Non-Indigenous Species

11. | What is the status of non-indigenous species and how is it changing?

Non-indigenous species are generally considered problematic and candidates for rapid response, if found, soon after invasion. For those that become established, their impacts can sometimes be assessed by quantifying changes in the affected native species. This question allows sanctuaries to report on the threat posed by non-indigenous species. In some cases, the presence of a species alone constitutes a significant threat (certain invasive algae). In other cases, impacts have been measured and may or may not significantly affect ecosystem integrity.

Good	Non-indigenous species are not suspected or do not appear to affect ecosystem integrity (full community development and function).
Good/Fair	Non-indigenous species exist, precluding full community development and function, but are unlikely to cause substantial or persistent degradation of ecosystem integrity.
Fair	Non-indigenous species may inhibit full community development and function and may cause measurable but not severe degradation of ecosystem integrity.
Fair/Poor	Non-indigenous species have caused or are likely to cause severe declines in some but not all ecosystem components and reduce ecosystem integrity.
Poor	Non-indigenous species have caused or are likely to cause severe declines in ecosystem integrity.

Living Resources
Key Species

12. | **What is the status of key species and how is it changing?**

Certain species can be defined as "key" within a marine sanctuary. Some might be keystone species, that is, species on which the persistence of a large number of other species in the ecosystem depends - the pillar of community stability. Their functional contribution to ecosystem function is disproportionate to their numerical abundance or biomass and their impact is therefore important at the community or ecosystem level. Their removal initiates changes in ecosystem structure and sometimes the disappearance of or dramatic increase in the abundance of dependent species. Keystone species may include certain habitat modifiers, predators, herbivores and those involved in critical symbiotic relationships (e.g. cleaning or co-habitating species).

Other key species may include those that are indicators of ecosystem condition or change (e.g., particularly sensitive species), those targeted for special protection efforts, or charismatic species that are identified with certain areas or ecosystems. These may or may not meet the definition of keystone, but do require assessments of status and trends.

Good   Key and keystone species appear to reflect pristine or near-pristine conditions and may promote ecosystem integrity (full community development and function).

Good/Fair   Selected key or keystone species are at reduced levels, perhaps precluding full community development and function, but substantial or persistent declines are not expected.

Fair   The reduced abundance of selected keystone species may inhibit full community development and function and may cause measurable but not severe degradation of ecosystem integrity; or selected key species are at reduced levels, but recovery is possible.

Fair/Poor   The reduced abundance of selected keystone species has caused or is likely to cause severe declines in some but not all ecosystem components, and reduce ecosystem integrity; or selected key species are at substantially reduced levels, and prospects for recovery are uncertain.

Poor   The reduced abundance of selected keystone species has caused or is likely to cause severe declines in ecosystem integrity; or selected key species are a severely reduced levels, and recovery is unlikely.

Living Resources
Health of Key Species

13. | **What is the condition or health of key species and how is it changing?**

For those species considered essential to ecosystem integrity, measures of their condition can be important to determining the likelihood that they will persist and continue to provide vital ecosystem functions. Measures of condition may include growth rates, fecundity, recruitment, age-specific survival, tissue contaminant levels, pathologies (disease incidence tumors, deformities), the presence and abundance of critical symbionts or parasite loads. Similar measures of condition may also be appropriate for other key species (indicator, protected or charismatic species). In contrast to the question about keystone species (#12 above), the impact of changes in the abundance or condition of key species is more likely to be observed at the population or individual level and less likely to result in ecosystem or community effects.

Good   The condition of key resources appears to reflect pristine or near-pristine conditions.

Good/Fair   The condition of selected key resources is not optimal, perhaps precluding full ecological function, but substantial or persistent declines are not expected.

Fair   The diminished condition of selected key resources may cause a measurable but not severe reduction in ecological function, but recovery is possible.

Fair/Poor   The comparatively poor condition of selected key resources makes prospects for recovery uncertain.

Poor   The poor condition of selected key resources makes recovery unlikely.

Living Resources
Human Activities

14. | **What are the levels of human activities that may influence living resource quality and how are they changing?**

Human activities that degrade living resource quality do so by causing a loss or reduction of one or more species, by disrupting critical life stages, by impairing various physiological processes, or by promoting the introduction of non-indigenous species or pathogens. (Note: Activities that impact habitat and water quality may also affect living resources. These activities are dealt with in Questions 4 and 8, and many are repeated here as they also have direct effect on living resources).

Fishing and collecting are the primary means of removing resources. Bottom trawling, seine-fishing and the collection of ornamental species for the aquarium trade are all common examples, some being more selective than others. Chronic mortality can be caused by marine debris derived from commercial or recreational vessel traffic, lost fishing gear and excess visitation, resulting in the gradual loss of some species.

Critical life stages can be affected in various ways. Mortality to adult stages is often caused by trawling and other fishing techniques, cable drags, dumping spoil or drill cuttings, vessel groundings or persistent anchoring. Contamination of areas by acute or chronic spills, discharges by vessels, or municipal and industrial facilities can make them unsuitable for recruitment; the same activities can make nursery habitats unsuitable. Although coastal armoring and construction can increase the availability of surfaces suitable for the recruitment and growth of hard bottom species, the activity may disrupt recruitment patterns for other species (e.g., intertidal soft bottom animals) and habitat may be lost.

Spills, discharges, and contaminants released from sediments (e.g., by dredging and dumping) can all cause physiological impairment and tissue contamination. Such activities can affect all life stages by reducing fecundity, increasing larval, juvenile, and adult mortality, reducing disease resistance, and increasing susceptibility to predation. Bioaccumulation allows some contaminants to move upward through the food chain, disproportionately affecting certain species.

Activities that promote introductions include bilge discharges and ballast water exchange, commercial shipping and vessel transportation. Releases of aquarium fish can also lead to species introductions.

Good	Few or no activities occur that are likely to negatively affect living resource quality.
Good/Fair	Some potentially harmful activities exist, but they do not appear to have had a negative effect on living resource quality.
Fair	Selected activities have resulted in measurable living resource impacts, but evidence suggests effects are localized, not widespread.
Fair/Poor	Selected activities have caused or are likely to cause severe impacts, and cases to date suggest a pervasive problem.
Poor	Selected activities warrant widespread concern and action, as large-scale, persistent and/or repeated severe impacts have occurred or are likely to occur.

Maritime Archaeological Resources Integrity

15. What is the integrity of known maritime archaeological resources and how is it changing?

The condition of archaeological resources in a marine sanctuary significantly affects their value for science and education, as well as the resource's eligibility for listing in the National Register of Historic Places. Assessments of archaeological sites include evaluation of the apparent levels of site integrity, which are based on levels of previous human disturbance and the level of natural deterioration. The historical, scientific and educational values of sites are also evaluated and are substantially determined and affected by site condition.

Good   Known archaeological resources appear to reflect little or no unexpected disturbance.

Good/Fair   Selected archaeological resources exhibit indications of disturbance, but there appears to have been little or no reduction in historical, scientific or educational value.

Fair   The diminished condition of selected archaeological resources has reduced, to some extent, their historical, scientific or educational value and may affect the eligibility of some sites for listing in the National Register of Historic Places.

Fair/Poor   The diminished condition of selected archaeological resources has substantially reduced their historical, scientific or educational value and is likely to affect their eligibility for listing in the National Register of Historic Places.

Poor   The degraded condition of known archaeological resources in general makes them ineffective in terms of historical, scientific or educational value and precludes their listing in the National Register of Historic Places.

Maritime Archaeological Resources Threat to Environment

16. Do known maritime archaeological resources pose an environmental hazard and how is this threat changing?

The sinking of a ship potentially introduces hazardous materials into the marine environment. This danger is true for historic shipwrecks as well. The issue is complicated by the fact that shipwrecks older than 50 years may be considered historical resources and must, by federal mandate, be protected. Many historic shipwrecks, particularly early to mid-20th century, still have the potential to retain oil and fuel in tanks and bunkers. As shipwrecks age and deteriorate, the potential for release of these materials into the environment increases.

Good   Known maritime archaeological resources pose few or no environmental threats.

Good/Fair   Selected maritime archaeological resources may pose isolated or limited environmental threats, but substantial or persistent impacts are not expected.

Fair   Selected maritime archaeological resources may cause measurable, but not severe, impacts to certain sanctuary resources or areas, but recovery is possible.

Fair/Poor   Selected maritime archaeological resources pose substantial threats to certain sanctuary resources or areas, and prospects for recovery are uncertain.

Poor   Selected maritime archaeological resources pose serious threats to sanctuary resources, and recovery is unlikely.

Maritime Archaeological Resources
Human Activities

17. | **What are the levels of human activities that may influence maritime archaeological resource quality and how are they changing?**

Some human maritime activities threaten the physical integrity of submerged archaeological resources. Archaeological site integrity is compromised when elements are moved, removed or otherwise damaged. Threats come from looting by divers, inadvertent damage by scuba diving visitors, improperly conducted archaeology that does not fully document site disturbance, anchoring, groundings, and commercial and recreational fishing activities, among others.

Good	Few or no activities occur that are likely to negatively affect maritime archaeological resource integrity.
Good/Fair	Some potentially relevant activities exist, but they do not appear to have had a negative effect on maritime archaeological resource integrity.
Fair	Selected activities have resulted in measurable impacts to maritime archaeological resources, but evidence suggests effects are localized, not widespread.
Fair/Poor	Selected activities have caused or are likely to cause severe impacts, and cases to date suggest a pervasive problem.
Poor	Selected activities warrant widespread concern and action, as large-scale, persistent, and/or repeated severe impacts have occurred or are likely to occur.

Appendix B: Consultation with Experts and Document Review

The process for preparing condition reports involves a combination of accepted techniques for collecting and interpreting information gathered from subject matter experts. The approach varies somewhat from sanctuary to sanctuary, in order to accommodate differing styles for working with partners. The Papahānaumokuākea Marine National Monument approach was closely related to the Delphi Method, a technique designed to organize group communication among a panel of geographically dispersed experts by using questionnaires, ultimately facilitating the formation of a group judgment. This method can be applied when it is necessary for decision-makers to combine the testimony of a group of experts, whether in the form of facts or informed opinion, or both, into a single useful statement.

The Delphi Method relies on repeated interactions with experts who respond to questions with a limited number of choices to arrive at the best supported answers. Feedback to the experts allows them to refine their views, gradually moving the group toward the most agreeable judgment. For condition reports, the Office of National Marine Sanctuaries uses 17 questions related to the status and trends of monument resources, with accompanying descriptions and five possible choices that describe resource condition.

In order to address the 17 questions, monument staff selected and consulted outside experts familiar with water quality, living resources, habitat, and maritime archaeological resources. A small workshop (around 10-20 participants) was convened where experts participated in facilitated discussions about each of the 17 questions. Experts represented various affiliations including Clancy Environmental Consultants, Hawai'i Department of Land and Natural Resources, Hawai'i Institute of Marine Biology, NOAA's Office of National Marine Sanctuaries, NOAA's Pacific Islands Fisheries Science Center, and the U.S. Fish and Wildlife Service. At the workshop each expert was introduced to the questions, was then asked to provide recommendations and supporting arguments, and the group supplemented the input with further discussion. In order to ensure consistency with Delphic methods, a critical role of the facilitator was to minimize dominance of the discussion by a single individual or opinion (which often leads to "follow the leader" tendencies in group meetings) and to encourage the expression of honest differences of opinion. As discussions progressed, the group converged in their opinion of the rating that most accurately describes the current resource condition. After an appropriate amount of time, the facilitator asked whether the group could agree on a rating for the question, as defined by specific language linked to each rating (see Appendix A). If an agreement was reached, the result was recorded and the group moved on to consider the trend in the same manner. If agreement was not reached, the facilitator instructed monument staff to consider all input and decide on a rating and trend at a future time, and to send their ratings back to workshop participants for individual comment.

The ratings and text found in the report are intended to summarize the opinions and uncertainty expressed by the experts, who based their input on knowledge and perceptions of local conditions.

Comments and citations received from the experts were included, as appropriate, in text supporting the ratings.

The first draft of the document was sent back to the subject experts for what was called an Initial Review, a 21-day period that allows them to ensure that the report accurately reflected their input, identify information gaps, provide comments or suggest revisions to the ratings and text. Upon receiving those comments, the writing team revised the text and ratings as they deemed appropriate. The final interpretation, ratings, and text in the draft condition report were the responsibility of monument staff, with final approval by the monument manager. To emphasize this important point, authorship of the report is attributed to the monument alone.   Subject experts were not authors, though their efforts and affiliations are acknowledged in the report.

The second phase of review, called Invited Review, involved particularly important partners in research and resource management, including NOAA's Marine Debris Program and NOAA's National Marine Fisheries Service. These bodies were asked to review the technical merits of resource ratings and accompanying text, as well as to point out any omissions or factual errors. The comments and recommendations of invited reviewers were received, considered by sanctuary staff, and incorporated, as appropriate, into a final draft document.

A draft final report was then sent to Dr. Jo-Ann Leong (Hawaii Institute of Marine Biology), Sam Pooley (Pacific Islands Fisheries Science Center) and Dan Polhemus (Hawaii State Department of Land and Natural Resources and the Bishop Museum) who served as external peer reviewers. This External Peer Review is a requirement that started in December 2004, when the White House Office of Management and Budget (OMB) issued a Final Information Quality Bulletin for Peer Review (OMB Bulletin) establishing peer review standards that would enhance the quality and credibility of the federal government's scientific information. Along with other information, these standards apply to Influential Scientific Information, which is information that can reasonably be determined to have a "clear and substantial impact on important public policies or private sector decisions." The Condition Reports are considered Influential Scientific Information. For this reason, these reports are subject to the review requirements of both the Information Quality Act and the OMB Bulletin guidelines. Therefore, following the completion of every condition report, they are reviewed by a minimum of three individuals who are considered to be experts in their field, were not involved in the development of the report, and are not ONMS employees. Comments from these peer reviews were incorporated into the final text of the report. Furthermore, OMB Bulletin guidelines require that reviewer comments, names, and affiliations be posted on the agency website: http://www.osec.doc.gov/cio/oipr/pr_plans.htm. Reviewer comments, however, are not attributed to specific individuals. Reviewer comments are posted at the same time as with the formatted final document.

Notes

www.ingramcontent.com/pod-product-compliance
Lightning Source LLC
Chambersburg PA
CBHW080444290526
45791CB00008BA/2605